Decisions at 15/16+

A guide to all your options

Susanne Christian

Student Helpbook Series

Lifetime
Publishing

Decisions at 15/16+ - A guide to all your options

Twelfth edition

Published by Lifetime Publishing, Mill House, Stallard Street, Trowbridge BA14 8HH

© Nord Anglia Lifetime Development South West Ltd, 2010

ISBN 978-1-904979-45-6

Cover design by Arthouse Creative

Illustrations by Royston Robertson

Printed in the EU by SS Media Ltd

The Career Development Organisation

CRAC: the career development organisation is an independent charity which encourages people to engage in career development and career-related learning. It seeks to support all those who help people with career decisions and is focused on providing them with expertise and innovation in careers information and learning. One of CRAC's recent innovations is icould - a freely accessible online database of 1000 personal career stories on film, told in their own words by individuals across the entire range of working sectors (www.icould.com).

Contents

About the author

Susanne Christian is an experienced careers adviser who has worked in schools, colleges, prisons and in the community helping adults and young people explore their options and move on in their lives.

Before becoming a careers adviser, Susanne worked in the Civil Service, for several voluntary organisations and as a local reporter on a forces newspaper overseas.

She now works freelance as a researcher, writer and editor for careers websites and writing careers books. She also spends time as a consultant and further education tutor and serves on the Adult Guidance Committee of the Institute of Career Guidance and the careers panel of the Financial Services Skills Council.

Acknowledgements

Thanks to Beryl Dixon, author of previous editions of *Decisions at 15/16+*, upon which this edition is based.

Thanks also to all those young people who have provided case studies for this edition (some names have been changed).

Chapter one

Life in year 11

Cast your mind back. Take a look at school life so far. Each year has been different. When you first went to secondary school everything was new, exciting and unexplored. By the beginning of year 8 you knew your way around. In year 9 you had important decisions to make about which exam subjects you were going to take after two more years. In year 10 you started to concentrate on those subjects.

Now it's the crunch year. You can't sail through this one and automatically move up to the next. There are big decisions to make. And they are in your hands now. Year 11 is your last compulsory year of full-time education. You may not want to stay at school. In any case, it might not be an option in your area if your school has no sixth form. Or you might want to move into some form of job-related education, at a further education college.

You might not want to stay in any form of full-time education at all, so you'll need to know what the alternatives are out there in the world of work. One thing is for sure – life is going to be quite different.

In 2009, the government passed laws for the Raising of the Participation Age (RPA), with the intention that those who started year 8 in 2009 will stay in education and training until the age of 17, and those who started year 7 in 2009 (and all younger students) will stay in education or training until 18. This doesn't necessarily mean you will have to stay on at school; it includes being in work-based learning, such as an Apprenticeship or in part-time education and training for those who are working (see Chapter seven).

The year ahead

How do you see it? Will it bring:

- freedom?
- choice?
- time to do what you want?
- no-one on your back?
- the end of homework – so free evenings?
- the chance to earn some money?

Forward planning

You will need to make sure that you do not miss any important dates and deadlines during the year. Now, this is probably the most packed year of your life so far. Most students in year 11 would probably claim that they have to squeeze far more into this year than ever before. You might agree with at least some of the students' comments on the next page.

These issues are common to most students, but that does not mean that everyone deals with them in exactly the same way. People deal with pressure differently. How do you manage your time and fit everything in? What about:

- planning and allowing plenty of time for coursework deadlines?
- balancing demands from different teachers?
- coping with exams and revision?
- how on earth to have any social life?
- finding time for a part-time job to earn some cash?

And on top of that you are expected to make decisions about your future?

There is so much to do that you will find it much easier if you draw up an action plan for the year. There is a calendar at the end of this chapter that summarises all the points you will need to think about. However, while a calendar like this is a useful guide, it is no substitute for a personal action plan in which you set out your ideas on where you are going and what you mean to do about getting there.

An action plan could include:

- your revision plans for the mock exams and for the real thing
- plans for completing coursework, highlighting the deadlines for handing it in, so you don't miss them
- important dates for applying for courses, jobs, etc
- dates of open days, taster days, etc you might want to go to.

Individual action planning brings these commitments into a recognisable framework so you can make sense of what is happening. In simple terms, an individual action plan asks some fundamental questions.

- Where am I now? – a realistic appreciation of your strengths.
- Where am I going? – a firm grasp of what is ahead.
- How do I get there? – careful planning of your objectives.
- How am I doing? – reviewing progress and setting new targets.

You might also want to keep a record of the advice and guidance you get to help you make your decisions about the next stage – for example, sessions with your Connexions personal adviser/careers adviser, PSHE careers sessions, assemblies, parents evenings or anything else that you have been to.

This will help you build up a picture of the pros and cons of any of the options you might be considering for next year and help you weigh up what will be right for you. If your school uses a Progress File or planner that could be useful here. Sometimes writing down all the information in one place can help you sort out your thoughts.

Decisions, decisions

No matter what anyone says, decision making is not easy. Good decisions cannot be made without information. To make a good decision you need the most up-to-date, relevant facts. You need to have discussions with other people and, above all, you need time to consider the benefits and disadvantages of each possible choice.

BUT you can't spend all this year thinking about your future. You still have to get the best end-of-year qualifications you can, in order to make that future happen. What about school work and exams?

Coping

Keep things in perspective

The student who enjoys doing every piece of set homework every night hasn't been born. Look at it this way: if homework and coursework were football, drama, going to discos or whatever your particular thing is, you would do it willingly. There are probably some subjects that you enjoy working at; others less so. This stage won't last for ever. BUT you need to get the best grades that you can in order to move on to the next stage. Then you can drop the dreaded maths/history/science/German, or whatever.

If you spend enough time on school work through the year you should get reasonable results. Exams are a way of measuring how far you have succeeded. They are designed to test what you know, understand and can do, not what you can't.

Things can easily get out of proportion. If exams, or any other problems, are getting you down, talk it over with people who on your side: teachers, parents or carers, friends or other advisers. There is always help and advice about – usually more than you think.

Good revision strategy

Everyone needs a sensible plan for revision. For some people, written exams at the end of this year will be the first big formal test that they have ever taken in certain subjects. In order to prepare for the real thing you need to feel what it is like to sit in silence for up to two hours separated from your friends in all directions by one to two metres. So you probably have mock exams. These will give you the chance to try out a revision plan. If you don't do as well in these exams as you had hoped, don't give up. They are intended to let you see how you get on and help you to learn from mistakes before you hit the real thing.

An important aim of your revision should be to identify your strengths and weaknesses. If you are revising for mock exams remember that they are a trial run, so that if you get it wrong there is a chance to put things right.

How have you got on in other tests over the years? You may have done SATS in year 9, or end-of-year exams in other years.

- Did you ever start revising too late to cover all the work required?
- Did you ever get distracted from your revision by demands from friends and family?
- Did you ever panic the night before the test?
- Did you ever stay up all night trying to catch up on revision?
- Did you ever get flustered on the day and write rubbish?
- Were you cross with yourself for losing marks?

The only way to deal with these problems is to PLAN your revision.

Six to eight weeks to go

It can help to write down all the subjects you have to revise, and add the date and time of the exam, and the type and length of exam for each subject. Then you can start to plan a revision timetable.

Be realistic about revision. It's hard. It's boring. You also have to revise on top of your normal workload. Draw up a checklist and hang it in your room by your books.

Subject	Exam title and number	Exam board	Coursework required	Date deadlines

Planning

You then need to get down to planning your subject revision calendar. One idea some people have found helpful is to choose combinations of subjects that demand different learning skills, so that you won't be bored; perhaps geography plus art, history plus science. Make sure you cover each subject at least twice during your revision, once early on and once nearer the exam.

Subject revision calendar	
Week 1	subjects A, B
Week 2	subjects C, D
Week 3	subjects E, F, A
Week 4	subjects G, H, C
Week 5	subjects B, D, E
Week 6	subjects F, G, H
Week 7	subjects A, B, C, D
Week 8	subjects E, F, G, H

It obviously makes sense to spend more time on the subjects you find hard – even if they're the subjects you like least.

Topics

You next need to identify topics within subjects. You can then see precisely what you should be doing in each of the revision weeks. Revision will not seem so daunting when you have broken the job down into easy stages.

Suggested examples

Science   Systems of the body

Plant functions

Structures and properties

Weather and atmosphere

Reactions

Electricity and magnetism

Forces and machines

Maths   Sets

Matrices

Scale drawings

Averages

Decimals

Volume

Angles

Graphs

That was the easy bit! Everyone likes preparing charts and timetables – especially on the computer. The problem comes in putting it into action.

If there were exam grades for lovingly prepared impressive, coloured and highlighted charts on bedroom walls, most people would get A* grades! It's translating the action plan into reality that is the hard part.

Revision techniques

When you have drawn up or printed off this beautiful timetable – how should you set about doing the revision? It should be *active* revision – in other words *doing* something – whether that's writing short outlines, making notes on topics, asking someone to listen to lists of facts or test vocabulary, practising exam answers or working through past papers. *Passive* revision means reading and re-reading something through, and hoping to remember it.

Everyone works differently. There is no single, off-the-shelf revision method that suits everyone. We all have different learning styles. Some people prefer to learn with words, others by diagrams and charts. Many people use a mixture of both, depending on the subject. There are some tried and tested techniques.

- Index cards – summaries of work neatly written on postcard-sized cards to fit into your pocket as quick reminders. You can use them to learn formulae, dates, vocabulary or quotations.

- Highlighting – go through your exercise books and files, and highlight the key passages and essential points. This provides you with a quick reference as you flick through your work.

- Flow diagrams – pictures can be easier to remember than words. You can pick out the main ideas, facts or arguments and link them with boxes, arrows or drawings. If they can describe a whole topic or illustrate a set of comparisons, they can be very helpful. They will also save time when you go back over your work.

- Trigger words – words that will trigger off your brain in the examination if they appear in the question. You can also use mnemonics to help you remember lists, such as the colours of the spectrum: Roses Of York Grow Better In Valleys (for Red, Orange, Yellow, Green, Blue, Indigo, Violet).

One approach that has been found useful is to pair up with a friend and for each of you to prepare different sections and then test each other on what you've learned.

Find the combination that suits you best. Your teachers will probably give you advice on revision too. They are experts. They have helped past year groups – and they have passed lots of exams themselves.

Concentration

Short periods of concentrated learning (not gazing out of the window!) followed by a short break are more effective than trying to do marathon stretches of revision. People will tell you that they did 20 hours of revision over the weekend, but they are fooling themselves. Effective studying is more important than the time you spend at your desk.

Testing yourself is also important, so that the material you have learned goes into your long-term memory. Giving yourself small treats can also be helpful. Promise yourself a break after you finish a topic or watch your favourite soap when you've finished a subject.

AND – tick off topics and subjects on your chart as you finish each one. Feel the glow of satisfaction.

Revision tips

- Pin up your revision timetable where you can't avoid seeing it.
- Plan breaks – and stick to them. *Move about,* even if it is only to get a hot or cold drink.
- Start with the subjects you *dislike or find harder.* Spend more time on them. Your favourite subjects will be easier.
- Stop work well before you go to bed or your brain will be churning all night.
- Nobody should revise for seven days a week.

This chapter contains only an outline of revision tips. You can find lots more – and plenty of help with individual subjects – on various websites, including:

- www.s-cool.co.uk
- www.revisioncentre.co.uk
- www.bbc.co.uk/schools/bitesize
- www.projectgcse.co.uk
- www.gcse.com

Important allies

Your parents or carers

Enlist your parents' or carers' support. Tell them about your arrangements. Now is the time to negotiate time off from jobs around the house if you can, since exams are the priority at this time.

Your friends

Look at the commitments you have outside school – friends, clubs and societies. Try to make sure they don't get in the way of work. Don't give up everything, because you will need a break from your revision, but strike a balance between work and leisure.

Exam time

- Check your exam timetable for dates and times carefully. You can't retake a missed exam.

- On the nights before examinations, get ready anything you'll need to take with you into the exam room – then go to bed early. Don't work right up to bedtime. You will perform better if you are fresh.

- In the morning, eat some breakfast. Your stomach needs something inside it.

- Get to school early. You'll be in a panic if you're late.

- Get to the exam on time.

During the exam

- Listen to the instructions read out in the exam hall.

- Make sure you know exactly how long you have for the exam.

- Read the instructions two or three times, so that you know – really know – what the examiner wants you to do. Don't write an answer to a question that isn't there, however much you would like to write about something that you know well!

- The examiners can only mark what you tell them, so don't leave blanks.

- Think and plan before you write.

- Don't be discouraged by the amount other students are writing. It could be rubbish.

- Make sure your planning leaves you enough time to answer the last questions properly.

- Use all the time given for the exam. Once you've left the exam you cannot add to your answers.

- Read through and check your answers. You'll have to leave a few minutes at the end for this.

After the exam, you'll want to talk to your friends about how it went. Don't be too put off by what they say they answered. It's a long time to wait until the results and it's too late for you to do anything about your answers!

Results

If you didn't do as well as expected in mock exams, don't panic. You now have time to put things right.

Ask yourself these questions.

- How well prepared was I really?

- Does the mark reflect fairly on my work?

- Where were the gaps in my knowledge?

- Did I pace myself well in the exam?

- Did I read the questions properly?

- Did I do the right number of questions in each section?

- Were there sections of work I found I did not understand?

> Note the gaps
>
> Make an action plan
>
> Ask teachers for help if necessary

If you are disappointed with your real exam results when the time comes, towards the end of August, don't despair. You can get help and advice on what to do next from your personal adviser/careers adviser.

Important point!

However confident you might be of your exam performance, it is a good idea not to be away on holiday when the results come out – just in case.

Year calendar

Here is the basic outline of a year calendar. Your school may have more deadlines or events for you to attend, so you can probably think of more points to add for yourself.

Autumn term

September, October

Start to look at all the options that will be available at the end of the year.

Talk to careers teachers and your personal adviser/careers adviser about possibilities for next year.

Attend open evenings at colleges of further education and sixth form colleges.

Collect leaflets about different courses available.

Check entry requirements to courses.

Look at the Apprenticeships website.

Make sure you know when all the closing dates are.

November, December

Start applying for courses. Some popular courses fill up very early so if you leave it too late places might have gone. If you apply now and change your mind later it won't matter. You can withdraw and someone else can have your place.

Spring term

January, February

Make a shortlist of jobs or Apprenticeships that interest you.

Find out about other jobs with training from your personal adviser/careers adviser.

Apply for jobs and Apprenticeships with early closing dates.

March

All coursework should be finished now.

Continue to make Apprenticeship and job applications.

Prepare for interviews, for jobs, Apprenticeships and courses.

Make an exam revision plan.

Summer term

April

Final revision.

Be sure to keep in touch with your careers/Connexions service so that they know which kinds of jobs or Apprenticeships interest you.

If you want a college place but have not applied yet, do it now.

May

If you are staying in education, see if you can arrange some work experience for part of the summer holidays.

GCSE exams start.

June

GCSE exams finish.

August

Results are out! Your plans for the next stage will be confirmed or not. It could be back to the drawing board, but don't panic – there is always help at hand! If you need any help after the exam results contact your careers/Connexions service.

Summary

- Year 11 is a year of change, with decisions to make.
- Plan out your time so you don't miss deadlines.
- You'll be more relaxed if you start revising in good time.

Chapter two

Are good grades all you need?

"Grades aren't everything – skills count too..."

Does your whole future depend on next summer's exams? Many students think so, but that's only part of the story. The qualifications you gain at the end of year 11 (or over the next few years) will be important, but there is more to getting and holding a job than good exam grades.

Qualifications count

We expect people who do a job for us to know what they are doing, especially if we are paying them or our safety depends on the job they do. Would you:

- want to have music lessons from someone who can't play that instrument?
- take your sick pet to a family friend instead of a qualified vet?
- buy a sandwich prepared by someone who doesn't know the importance of clean hands?
- let a friend without a licence teach you to drive?

In other words, you expect people to be qualified to do the job.

School qualifications are an important first stage. The grades you get should reflect the level of skill and knowledge you have developed, and the teachers, trainers and employers who will be concerned with your next and later stages will be very interested in seeing just how good you are. Your grades provide one way for colleges and businesses to assess your potential as a future student or employee.

When your results come out in the summer, you will have achieved at one or more of these levels for your GCSEs.

Grade A* – shows exceptional quality.

Grades A, B, C – the higher grades needed for some training programmes and jobs, and for further and higher education.

Grades D, E – regarded as average grades, a good base from which to grow.

Grades F, G – the lower, but still useful, grades of achievement.

Ungraded – unfortunately, no score.

These exams will have indicated what you know thoroughly, understand and can do. But your results are based on more than just what your memory can produce in the exam room. The coursework, projects and other assignments you tackled during the year will have counted towards the final grade you received. The proportion of your final mark that depends on coursework will vary between subjects and examination boards.

Skills count too

We live in an increasingly complex world (more about this in Chapter three). Because of this you need a certain level of skills just to deal with day-to-day life:

- looking for information on the internet

- filling in an online application form
- deciding which mobile phone package is best for you
- following the instructions to set up a new piece of equipment
- reading safety instructions on a packet of hair colour
- applying for a provisional driving licence or theory test.

And that's before you think about what you might need for a job!

The people who will eventually give you a job want more than certificates. They may well ask for exam passes in certain subjects but they will also want a selection of what are known as transferable skills – those that can be required in many different jobs. They could be looking for someone who is good at accepting responsibility, a good planner, able to work well with other people and so on.

There are some very important **social skills** that are needed to get on with people.

- Skills in personal relations – this includes seeing the issue from the other person's standpoint, cooperating towards an agreed objective and the ability to get on with others whose views differ from yours, while keeping your own values. (See Jo, Billy, Laura, Anil, Leanne and their bosses later in this chapter.)

- Skills in communication – such as the ability to set out ideas clearly in words and diagrams, used for writing reports or drawing up plans and the ability to express yourself orally and take part in discussions.

Then there are **technical skills** used mainly with equipment and in activities.

- Skills in numeracy – such as the ability to use numerically based information, including statistics, graphs, flow charts, spreadsheets and mathematical models, and skills of estimation, calculation and projection.

- Skills in applied technology – including using the internet, hardware and software to store and retrieve information, analyse problems and apply solutions to them.

There are lots of surveys of employers asking what are the skills and qualities they look for in employees. Most of them say the same sorts of things. The list looks something like this:

- analytical ability – doesn't jump to the first solution that presents itself
- commercial awareness – knows what makes money and what saves money
- communication – can explain things clearly, in speech and writing
- confidence – relates to all types of people, is honest and open
- dedication – does what's needed to get the job done
- determination – won't back off if the situation gets tough
- drive and energy – the ability to get things done
- enquiring mind – willingness to ask questions
- honesty and integrity – takes responsibility for own actions
- listening skills – understands and takes account of other points of view
- motivation and enthusiasm – willingness to do a bit extra
- pride in the job – attentive to detail
- reliability – will turn up and ensure the job is done.

Functional skills

Some skills are very specific to a particular job or career area and you probably won't need those skills unless you do that job. Other skills are much more generalised and you need them in lots of different walks of life.

You won't get far today unless you have a certain level of:

- English
- ICT
- maths.

These skills are so crucial they are needed by everyone. These are known as functional skills. If something is 'functional' it means it's useful, it works. So functional skills are what you need to be effective – at work and in the modern world. Everyone needs them.

They will form part of the work-related or work-based learning options you may choose at 16+, including Apprenticeships and Diplomas (see Chapters six and seven). Because this sort of education is very practically based, the functional skills will be taught in a very practical way that relates them to uses in the real world. Some of these will be related to your chosen vocational area and others will apply across all areas, such as filling in application forms.

(There have been functional skills pilot schemes running in some areas, so people who have already taken qualifications in these pilots may not have to take them again.)

Skills

Alongside the functional skills we need other skills.

Ask yourself...

- How many times have you been annoyed by a shop assistant who has given you poor service?

- Would you like to be treated by a doctor who snaps your head off every time you go to the surgery?

- Did you regret going down to the market to buy that cheap watch, which has already packed in?

- Have you ever nearly been mown down on a zebra crossing by a lorry driver in a hurry who did not want to stop?

- Have you ever been kept waiting at an enquiry desk while the receptionist chatted on the phone?

- Is it worth going to the cinema if the staff always challenge you rudely about your age?

This is not to suggest that all shop assistants don't care, doctors don't take time, market traders are dishonest, lorry drivers are inconsiderate, receptionists are rude or cinema staff surly. But these things can and do happen. Every time these situations do occur, they remind us that there is more to doing a job than being qualified for it. Attitudes are very important.

Qualifications may open doors to opportunities. Skills are needed to survive when you get there. Think about the following skills:

- asserting yourself with confidence

- assessing other people's capabilities
- being responsible towards other people
- calculating your effect on other people
- chairing a committee meeting
- communicating with other people
- controlling your temper
- dealing with injustice
- driving a vehicle
- estimating accounts
- first aid skills
- getting a job
- getting information
- getting other people's cooperation
- giving information
- handling money
- interpreting plans
- IT skills
- listening to others
- making decisions
- making friends
- organising your time
- persuading other people
- planning
- problem solving
- resisting pressure from other people
- resisting provocation
- seeing things from another person's point of view
- separating fact from prejudice

- speaking at a public meeting
- taking orders
- taking the initiative
- using a telephone
- working in a team
- writing a report.

We use and develop our skills all the time. Just living our lives uses skills from the list every day. Have a look at this story.

Sasha's eventful day

Sasha rushed downstairs to get the post. It was there – the letter she was waiting for about the summer holiday job she had applied for **(getting a job)***. Good news, they were inviting her for an interview, but on a day when she had an exam. 'Oh no' she said to her mum, 'I'll have to miss the interview. I wanted that job. How come it happens like this? Don't they know it's exam time?' Even though she was so upset, Sasha heard her mum's suggestion* **(listening to others)** *that she try phoning to ask if the interview time could be changed. She wasn't sure about doing that but decided if she wanted the job she had to try* **(making decisions)***.*

Sasha phoned the number on the letter **(getting information)** *and asked for the manager who sent the letter* **(using the telephone)***. When he answered she said 'Hallo Mr Salman. Thank you for your letter about the interview. I'm afraid I can't come at 2pm as I have an exam that afternoon'* **(asserting yourself with confidence)** *'I could come in the morning'* **(problem solving)***. 'Thanks', said Mr Salman, '11am?' 'That would be fine', replied Sasha* **(communicating with people)***.*

When Sasha told her mum, she said 'That means I can't use the morning for last-minute revision **(planning ahead)***. I'll have to make sure I do it all the day before'* **(organising your time)***.*

The front door opened. It was Sasha's little brother Linus. He had a dog with him. 'Whose dog's that?' asked Sasha. 'I found him wandering on the road' said Linus. 'He's got an address on him.'

Sasha looked at the tag **(getting information)**. *It was across the main road so she thought she'd better go as well* **(assessing other people's capabilities)**.

Sasha had a look on the internet to check the best route to the dog owner's house **(IT skills)**. *As they were walking round the corner, a man said to them 'What're you doing with my dog? Trying to steal him?' and took him from Linus roughly. 'We were bringing him home to you', said Sasha* **(dealing with injustice)** *trying hard to stay calm* **(keeping your temper)**. *'Another time, leave him alone', said the man. Sasha was tempted to say something back, but she just took Linus back home* **(resisting provocation)**. *'He was probably worried about the dog', she said as they walked back home* **(seeing things from another person's point of view)**.

Later, it was time for football practice. When Sasha got there, she found there was a new team member. As captain, Sasha made sure she said hallo **(making friends)**. *The coach introduced her. 'Niquita has been playing for the Hornets. I want to try her as a striker. So Sasha you're on the bench for this game.' Sasha was upset. That seemed unfair. One of her friends said, 'She can't just walk in and take your position. She can't be that good. My brother says the Hornets are all talk and no results.' But Sasha said, 'I know, it's unfair. I've played so well this season. But you know the Hornets won the trophy last season* **(separating fact from prejudice)** *so we have to listen to the coach* **(taking orders)** *and give her a chance. Maybe it'll be good for the team'* **(teamwork)**.

A whole range of social and life skills was at work there. They can be hard to spot and we don't always realise that we're using them all the time.

Looking ahead

Think about life beyond school. There will be a whole range of people to get on with and situations to deal with in the workplace. If you have a part-time job you may already have come across some of these situations.

Consider the following questions.

Are you willing to learn new things?

Everyone likes to feel secure. If you are successful in a job well within your skills, this can be very satisfying. It will not last for ever. Moving on will mean going beyond the familiar things you know you can cope with. New demands can bring insecurity if you don't prepare yourself, but there are training opportunities, which will prevent you feeling threatened.

Are you prepared to make allowances for difficult workmates?

Unless you plan on being a hermit, every job will bring with it a collection of colleagues. They will not be perfect. They will have their own peculiar ways. They will expect you to fit in and may resent the new recruit. How you handle this will be crucial. The way you get on with others at school will tell you whether you have problems ahead.

Are you prepared to go beyond what is asked for?

These days most occupations have job descriptions, so it should be clear what is expected of you. There are no rules, however, that prevent you going the extra mile or going out of your way to be helpful. The company that takes more care is the one that is likely to attract more business. And that's your job assured.

Are you willing to accept responsibility?

Being part of a business means taking a share in some level of responsibility. How you react to this is certain to affect a whole range of activities undertaken by many others. If you have the skill and a positive attitude, extra responsibility can be welcome in terms of job satisfaction.

Do you accept unpleasant tasks willingly?

Life is rarely one great social whirl. Every job has its boring bits. You are going to have to decide whether to skimp on the distasteful parts or to accept them willingly. Your boss will be very interested to see how you cope – whether you take them in your stride or moan endlessly. Your ultimate promotion could depend on your attitude to the dull and repetitive parts of your work.

Do you recognise your own weaknesses?

Nobody's perfect, but if you pretend to other people that you are, it will land you in trouble. If you make a mistake, be open about it. Admitting your error before it is discovered by the boss is a positive approach, which people will appreciate. If you have done something that justifies criticism, accepting it without going into a sulk is a useful skill to have.

Seeing things from another person's point of view

Here are some more work situations to think about.

Jo says:

'I'm stuck in this job. No one pays any attention to me. I'll never get anywhere.'

Her boss says:

'She never shows any real interest or enthusiasm for her work, so I don't think I will promote her.'

WHO IS RIGHT?

Billy says:

'I'm bored with my job. It's dull and I want something more interesting to do.'

His boss says:

'He wants to push ahead too fast. He hasn't even mastered the skills of his present job.'

WHO IS RIGHT?

Laura says:

'He always tells me the mistakes I've made. He never says anything about the good things.'

Her boss says:

'She drives me crazy, making the same mistakes over and over again. Does she never learn?'

WHO IS RIGHT?

Anil says:

'She's so fussy when I come in a few minutes late in the morning, even when I'm willing to stay later in the afternoon.'

His boss says:

'He doesn't know the meaning of punctuality. He thinks he can be late whenever he wants to and make it up at the end of the day when he's not needed.'

WHO IS RIGHT?

Leanne says:

'I've been on the same machine for a year now. It's high time they put me on to something else.'

Her boss says:

'She's only been here a year and wants to go on to something else – just when she's getting useful to me.'

WHO IS RIGHT?

The difficulty with some problems is that they depend more on the way we see things than on what really happens. Jo, Billy, Laura, Anil and Leanne and their bosses each make statements about the same situation, but they're only seeing it from their own point of view. Unless they sort themselves out, there's trouble looming. To resolve the problems, they need to start communicating and putting themselves in each other's shoes. Being able to see the situation from the other person's point of view is an important skill for all of us.

Summary

- Qualifications count, but you need skills as well.
- You are developing and using skills every day.
- Be aware of your own strengths and weaknesses.

Chapter three

Visions of the future

"I think your future is in computers..."

CLICK TO PROCEED
OK

The employment situation in the UK is affected by economic factors, both here and across the rest of the world. Within the UK, it varies across regions and in different occupational areas.

Changing world of work

In the past 20 or 30 years (since your parents or carers were your age) there have been huge changes in the world of work – some have been gradual changes and some have been quite drastic and unexpected.

- Fewer people have a 'job for life'. Instead of joining a company after school, college or university and staying there until retirement, most people these days expect to move jobs much more frequently.

- It is quite common for people nowadays to change careers several times in their working lives.

- Many jobs are on fixed-term contracts rather than permanent.

- Over one million people have several part-time jobs, adding up to 'portfolio careers'.

- Small businesses run from home account for more than 25% of UK employment. Some of these are run alongside full- or part-time paid employment.

Jobs change. Automation has led to a drop in the number of manual and semi-skilled jobs. The growth and application of technology has made some skills unnecessary and put others in great demand. Thirty years ago, the following activities and kinds of equipment were only being planned:

- automatic cash dispensing machines

- bar codes

- body scanners

- computer-marked exams

- desktop publishing

- electronic news gathering

- home computers

- keyhole surgery

- mobile telephones

- pocket calculators

- robots

- weather satellites.

Even in the last few years things have changed. Just look at the development of Web 2.0 and all that it's brought – social networking, viral marketing, digital advertising and so on.

Your grandparents may have worked in jobs that no longer exist in their original form. They have either disappeared altogether or have been changed into other kinds of work. The job of draughtsman/woman, for instance, has changed dramatically. Thirty years ago there were huge offices full of skilled people doing manual drawings for engineers, architects and surveyors. Technology has transformed that job. Now skilled technicians use computer-aided design (CAD) in their work. That is an example of a job that has changed.

Twenty years ago who had heard of web designers, call centre assistants or personal trainers? These are examples of completely new jobs.

Other changes have been quicker and more dramatic. Of course, the world economic recession has been the most important recent event to affect people's working lives. At the time of writing (2010), unemployment is the highest it's been for 15 years at over 1.5 million, with only half a million advertised vacancies. Even worse is the fact that unemployment for young people is the highest it's ever been.

Some of the people who have recently been made redundant had been working in the same job or company for 20, 30 or more years. It is hard for them to change to another career area or retrain for a different job.

Facing competition

But it's not all bad news. The recession won't last for ever. It is important to be ready when it comes to an end.

The technological changes outlined above have led to changes in the demand for skills – more skilled people are needed and with skills at a higher level. So there is more demand for people at professional and technician level. The way to achieve this is through acquiring skills at the appropriate level – usually through a degree, HND or professional qualification (Chapter ten has more information on how this applies to different career areas).

All this adds up to the fact that everyone has to make sure they are giving themselves the best chance of being able to compete in the job market. This means having the right qualifications and skills as well as being flexible and willing to accept changes. The future belongs to people who have the right qualifications and skills, and who are prepared to be flexible and retrain as necessary.

Even people who stay in the same job area or profession need to keep developing their skills and knowledge just to stay up to date. In fact many occupations have a system of annual updates called continuing professional development (CPD). Nurses, doctors, surveyors and teachers, for example, all have to show that they have undertaken CPD.

What will the world of work really be like?

Different from school, that's for sure. At whatever age you enter the labour market, whether that's 16, 18 or 21+, full-time work is going to be a big change. It will be interesting... perhaps not all the time. It will certainly be a new challenge. The best way to meet a challenge and deal with it successfully is to be prepared.

You will be moving towards independence in many ways. One of the most important is by earning your own money.

You're in charge

Being self-employed is a popular choice these days – in 2009, it was estimated that over four million people worked for themselves. You could consider setting up your own business. You need a good idea and probably some money to get you set up. There are places where young people can get business advice and sometimes funding.

- Shell LiveWIRE
- The Prince's Trust
- Business Link.

These organisations have funded business ideas by young people which include:

- diaries for nurses
- fairly traded coffee
- specialist food suppliers
- sustainable furniture
- tropical fish breeding
- cycle repairs
- glass design
- photography.

It's worth thinking about. Chapter twelve has contact details and more information.

Work experience

It's a valuable step on the way towards the world of work. Maybe you have already done a placement in year 10 or year 11?

Most people naturally see work experience as an opportunity to try out the kind of job they think that they might want to go into – and that is obviously a priority. Even if you can't get work experience in your chosen area, it's still valuable.

And if you don't really have any clear career ideas yet, work experience can help you decide what kind of work you want to do – or even what you don't want to do! For some people work experience showed them a job that they didn't know about or didn't know they'd enjoy.

Wherever you go, you will experience working with other people, observing how they react with one another, what kind of problems might crop up and how they are resolved. You'll work with some people you like and some you don't (but will learn to get on with). You'll learn about health and safety, see how different managers and supervisors get the best out of people (or don't) and how people divide their time in the workplace. You'll be able to draw on all this later when you are filling in job application forms or answering questions at interviews. So, if your first choice of work experience placement isn't available, don't automatically think that nothing else will do. All work experience gives an insight into work.

If you stay in full-time education next year you should get the opportunity to do a further work experience placement. If you are going on to do a vocational course you will almost certainly do several placements, as they will form an important part of the course. If you choose an academic course, work experience might still be on offer – or you might get the chance of work shadowing.

Work shadowing

In your work experience placement you probably had a go at the job. Well, there are many jobs where this just wouldn't be practicable. After all, you wouldn't expect to take part in heart surgery, plead in court or drive a high-speed train. So work shadowing is usually appropriate when it's still important for students to get a flavour of a job, but can't do it hands on. What they can do, though, is observe. This makes shadowing sound boring, but it need not be. You can ask questions. The person being shadowed will normally take time to explain what they are doing and why. You might even be able to take part to a certain extent. Students have successfully shadowed, for example:

- Members of Parliament (MPs) – who have allowed them to sit in on meetings and surgeries for constituents

- solicitors – who have taken them to observe the workings of a court

- business managers – who have shown them the day-to day running of the business.

(Of course, in any profession, sitting in on client discussions has to be with the client's consent.)

There are some jobs that are almost impossible to enter unless you have done some relevant work experience or shadowing. This is because they are particularly demanding, either physically, mentally or both. The people who organise training courses for these professions want to know that students who apply really know what's involved. Spending some time shadowing also shows that you are really committed to the work.

Examples include:

- agriculture

- social work

- teaching

- medicine

- dentistry

- veterinary work

- healthcare professions such as physiotherapy and occupational therapy.

If you decide to go into full-time higher education (university or college of higher education) when you are 18, you will find that work experience may be on offer again. It will almost certainly be provided on vocational courses. Many students on other courses arrange to spend part of the holidays shadowing or gaining work experience.

Of course you may be in paid work already – at weekends or in the holidays. Even if this is not related to your career choice, it is still valuable experience. You will be learning all sorts of work-related skills. Other employers will appreciate the head start you have over someone who's never worked.

And if you are doing any voluntary work then this will interest employers too.

Grant changed his career plans after getting a Christmas job

'I stayed on in the sixth form at school and resat my maths and English GCSEs. I applied for an Apprenticeship in engineering but couldn't get a place. I got a Christmas job in a record shop and really loved it. When that came to an end I really didn't want to leave. What I liked was being with adults. I know a bit about music so I enjoyed talking to the customers. We'd have some good discussions. It was busy, though, in the run up to Christmas. I didn't mind that, it's better to be busy. I've seen what it's like in a shop with the long hours. I'd like to be a store manager and see my store achieve the top sales figures. I'm at college on a retail course and I've applied for a part-time job back at the record shop.'

Deciding on the right route for the future

So you are on the point of having some choices to make from a wide range of alternatives. It's your choice. A great deal depends on your personality and interests. You decide on the right course of action for you. Try this checklist to get your answers into focus.

- Has my career choice an entry route at 18+ or 21+?
- What level of qualifications is the usual route for entry into the career area of my choice?
- Do I want to stay at school or is it time for a change?
- Could I study one, two or three subjects to A level standard?
- Am I interested in higher education?
- Are there new subjects that attract me?
- What about an applied A level?
- Are there any subjects that I previously dropped and would like to take up again?

- Would I be much more suited to learning while earning in work with training?

You're not on your own

You don't have to make all these decisions completely on your own. Remember that they are your decisions, though, and don't be influenced by what your friends are doing or what people say you should do unless you have reason to respect their advice.

There are sources of help available. These are described in the next chapter.

Summary

- The world is changing fast – old jobs are going and new ones are being created.

- People who are flexible in their careers are going to be most successful.

- Work experience, paid or unpaid, of any type is useful.

Chapter four

Which way now?

Routes ahead

As you can see from the first three chapters, year 11 is just a stage on a longer journey, which has some way to run. GCSEs are not the end of the road – they are launch pads to what is to come. The demands of the world of work are driving things that way.

Remember your choices at 14+? You made those in year 9, when you were deciding what to study in years 10 and 11. That probably seemed hard enough. Some of your choices were familiar subjects, with perhaps some new ones on offer. Most of the study was based in school –

although some vocational subjects, particularly the new Diplomas, are taught outside school.

Choosing at 16+ is different because there are far more options. You can choose between:

- full-time study – studying towards general, academic qualifications
- full-time study – towards work-related qualifications
- full-time study – with a combination of general, academic and career-related qualifications
- employment with training
- an Apprenticeship.

Chapter five looks at general (academic) education, Chapter six covers work-related education and Chapter seven is about work-based learning.

You will also have a choice about where to go for the choices you make, whether that's further studies or employment. These include:

- your school
- a different school
- sixth form college
- further education college
- an employer.

Some of the choices are made for you – if you want to work, you need an employer. Others are for you to decide. There is more about these choices and how to make them in Chapter eight.

The chart on the next page shows your choices.

Try this quiz to see which one might suit you.

Would you like to:

1.

    a) Continue your general education next year to keep all options open?

    b) Move on to a full-time work-related course?

    c) Gain work-related qualifications while in employment?

    d) Get a well-paid job?

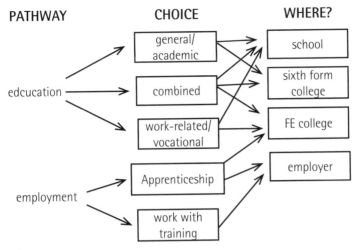

PATHWAY	CHOICE	WHERE?
edcucation	general/ academic	school
	combined	sixth form college
	work-related/ vocational	FE college
employment	Apprenticeship	employer
	work with training	

2.

a) Continue in full-time learning?

b) Continue with a full-time course only if what you do seems relevant to a career?

c) Study part time, perhaps through time off from work to attend courses?

d) Enough's enough. You've had enough of school work and homework?

3.

a) Stay at school or move to a full-time college course?

b) Take a full-time course that will lead to a job in one or two years' time?

c) Get qualifications, assisted by an employer?

d) Earn a wage?

4.

a) Go to university, eventually?

b) Go to a specialist college (e.g. a college of music, technology or drama)?

c) Go to evening classes if necessary to get high-level work-related qualifications?

d) Forget qualifications. You can always change job if you need more money?

Answers

If you answered:

Mainly (a) The full-time education option is the one for you – and you'll keep your options open rather than make a career choice right now.

Mainly (b) You'll choose to stay on a full-time course if it relates to your future career.

Mainly (c) You'd like to get more qualifications – and have some money coming in at the same time.

Mainly (d) You would prefer to start work immediately and preferably get a well-paid job.

So those answers determine what you will do from now on? No. Nothing you decide now will be fixed for ever. There will be lots of opportunities to change your route during the next few years. Don't worry that decisions taken during this year will commit you forever to one pathway.

Changing your mind

You could follow one route and later transfer to another. For instance:

- you decide to go back to college after a year in work

- you start the sixth form but decide that you'd rather be at college

- you go to college but decide you'd rather be working and earning

- you start an academic course but decide you'd prefer vocational subjects.

The whole point about today's courses and qualifications is that they are designed to be flexible. If you have gone down one route and it turns out to be not what you expected or not what you want to do then you can change to a different route. You may have to wait until the following September, as most courses run from September to June. Joining most courses part way through is not usually allowed as you will have missed too much of the work.

There is more about how different qualifications relate to each other later in this chapter.

Before you start to make any decisions it's worth considering that:

- employers say they would pay an extra £2,261 a year for those with five GCSEs at grades A*-C – on average £13,016 compared with £11,412 for those with just one GCSE

- statistics show that people with five GCSEs earn an average of £55 a week more than those without

- employers say they would pay £450 more for every GCSE

- five GCSEs, or equivalent level 2 qualifications, are 'worth £1m over a lifetime' – people with level 2 qualifications earn an average of £1,022,112 compared with £873,392 over a working lifetime for those with no qualifications..

(All figures from 2007, based on data from the Office for National Statistics.)

Why go to work?

You might choose to get a job. In some parts of the country this can be difficult. As we saw in Chapter three, current (2010) employment has hit young people particularly hard and there are fewer jobs for untrained people. This means that if you are offered a job, especially if the money is good, it is going to be very tempting to take it.

It is worth finding out about a bit about the job besides the pay. Some jobs are likely to lead to more of a future than others. There is a difference between a job that involves training and a job without, especially if it's recognised, accredited training.

Most jobs include some initial training – about the company and its systems, who everyone is and where to find things. But in some jobs that's all you get.

The trouble with a job that doesn't include accredited training is that you may find you are doing exactly the same thing in a year or two's time as you were on day one. Apart from anything else this may mean that you are earning no more than you were when you started. Remember that the salary may be tempting now, but will it be so good a few years on when you have financial commitments – like rent to pay or you want to buy a car?

A job with recognised training is likely to offer better prospects, the chance to take some responsibility or even be promoted.

So it's worth keeping an eye on the future even when you're starting out. Remember that if you are 16 or 17 and haven't yet got a level 2 qualification (such as 5 GCSEs at grades A*-C), you are entitled to time off for study or training (see Chapter seven). Even if the employer doesn't offer training, you could ask for it. But it's worth asking before you take the job rather than waiting until you're already there.

Before you decide on the work option you may like to ask yourself these questions.

- How easy it is to find work near where you live? Are there lots of opportunities, or is there high unemployment?

- Which employers in your area recruit and train school leavers?

- What kinds of jobs do they offer and what are the future prospects?

- What entry qualifications do they want – exam passes or other skills?

- Is training included or would you have to arrange your own?

Why stay in education?

There are several possible reasons.

- You feel that higher qualifications could improve your job prospects.

- You know that you will need A levels to enter the career of your choice.

- You want to go to university or a college of higher education.

- You need more than GCSEs to get the job you want.

- You haven't made a career choice yet and want more time to decide.

- You want to start learning about an area of work while you are still at school or college.

Nowadays you don't have to make a straight choice between academic, general education – such as A levels or the International Baccalaureate (IB) – or career-related courses. It is now much more possible to mix and match from the different types of qualification on offer.

So, you do not have to stick with one kind of award. Qualifications and learning programmes are becoming so flexible that you can mix and match according to your own preference. (But do take advice on the suitability of what you choose.) And REMEMBER that not all subjects or combinations of subjects are available at all schools and colleges.

The combinations are almost limitless. How about:

- a general, academic AS/A level with a double-award applied A level?
- two general AS/A levels with three GCSEs?
- an A level and a BTEC Award?
- level 3 Diploma and an A level?
- the IB and ECDL?
- AS/A levels with a business administration course?
- two general AS/A levels with a wordprocessing course?
- AS/A levels plus an NVQ in sport and recreation?

Becky is doing a 12-unit A level in applied health and social care with one general A level

'I could have chosen general A levels and I did think about doing biology, sociology and psychology because they would also have been useful in the health and social care fields. I've always wanted to do something in care or a profession related to medicine. But I decided that if I did a double-award A level in applied health and social care plus a general one I could have the best of both worlds – study the subjects that interest me and get some hands-on experience as well. So I chose health and social care and am also doing A level psychology.

I'm really enjoying the applied course. The assignments are very interesting. For 'Physical aspects of health' I've had to do a spreadsheet to make charts showing how diseases are spread – by contamination, by direct contact with people, or airborne. As the news was full of the possible bird flu epidemic at the time it was incredibly interesting. For another one I had to investigate provision of primary health care in the area. The group assignments are good because we learn to work together. At first we found it difficult to work out which of us would do each topic, but now we have learned how to divide up the work equally and negotiate over who does what.

I think that I want to be a paediatric nurse so I shall be sure to take child development and childcare practice as two of my options. I will also ask my course tutor to arrange for me to do some work experience in a children's ward. We will study some of the health professional careers later on in the course, so I might change my mind.'

Jack is doing a general A level in theatre studies together with a six-unit A level in applied business

'I didn't want to do the business bit but so many people gave me horror stories about 'resting' (unemployed) actors that I gave in to pressure. I reasoned that I could always fall back on accountancy or something if necessary...

I could have gone to a different college to do a BTEC National qualification in performing arts (acting) but I chose this course because I wanted to study some set texts as well as do the practical side – and I am enjoying the two plays we have to study in depth. However, I also love being in front of an audience. I audition for all the college productions and nearly always get a part even if it isn't the lead. I also belong to an amateur group, which has a very good reputation locally. Our shows always sell out. Through this I've gained experience in singing and in things we share, like front-of-house management and ticket sales. And I prompt. That's a skill in itself and one that some people find tricky.'

However, Jack has recently decided against trying to make it as a performer.

'I'm quite realistic. I'm no better than thousands of others out there. So I have decided to keep drama as a hobby and put a lot of time into a local theatre group wherever I end up living. What I want to do is teach primary school children. A group of us worked with some primary school children last year for our major project. We had to coach and direct them in a play. I really enjoyed that and found that I related to the children easily. I was worried that I might need an A

level subject but I've been told that I should be all right as I have nine good GCSEs in a spread of subjects. My performance skills should help me in the classroom and I'll be able to teach dance and drama to all the year groups. So I still don't need the business training! But at least I have one more career option if I decide against teaching as well.'

How do qualifications relate to each other?

There are so many qualifications around that it can be quite confusing. It may make it difficult to decide which is the right one for you. There have been some recent changes designed to make the whole system a bit easier to understand.

National Qualifications Framework (NQF)

All qualifications are now graded so they fit into one of nine levels. This chart overleaf shows you how the levels relate to each other.

You can see from the chart that if you get five GCSEs at grades A*-C, you will enter the chart at level 2. If your GCSE grades are D-G, you will be at level 1.

Many of the choices you are making at 16 will involve study at level 3. This is the most usual level of qualifications required for university entry.

Vocational qualifications fit into these levels, too. This is the most recent change to this system.

NQF level	Examples of qualifications	What they give you/who they are for
Entry	• Entry level certificates	• basic knowledge and skills • ability to apply learning in everyday situations • not geared towards specific occupations
1	• GCSEs grades D-G • BTEC Introductory Diplomas and Certificates • NVQs at level 1	• basic knowledge and skills • ability to apply learning with guidance or supervision • may be linked to job competence
2	• GCSEs grades A*-C • BTEC First Diplomas and Certificates • NVQs at level 2	• good knowledge and understanding of a subject • ability to perform a variety of tasks with some guidance or supervision • appropriate for many job roles
3	• A levels • Advanced Extension Awards • A levels in applied subjects • International Baccalaureate • NVQs at level 3 • BTEC Diplomas, Certificates and Awards • BTEC Nationals • OCR Nationals	• ability to gain or apply a range of knowledge, skills and understanding, at a detailed level • appropriate if you plan to go to university, work independently, or (in some cases) supervise and train others in their field of work
4	• NVQs at level 4 • BTEC Professional Diplomas, Certificates and Awards	• specialist learning, involving detailed analysis of a high level of information and knowledge in an area of work or study • appropriate for people working in technical and professional jobs, and/or managing and developing others

5	• HNCs and HNDs • NVQs • BTEC Professional Diplomas, Certificates and Awards	• increased depth of knowledge and understanding of an area of work or study, so you can respond to complex problems and situations • high level of work expertise and competence in managing and training others • appropriate for people working as higher grade technicians, professionals or managers
6	• National Diploma in Professional Production Skills • BTEC Advanced Professional Diplomas, Certificates and Awards	• a specialist, high-level knowledge of an area of work or study, to enable you to use your own ideas and research in response to complex problems and situations • appropriate for people working as knowledge-based professionals or in professional management positions
7	• Diploma in Translation • BTEC Advanced Professional Diplomas, Certificates and Awards	• highly developed and complex levels of knowledge, enabling you to develop original responses to complicated and unpredictable problems and situations • appropriate for senior professionals and managers
8	• specialist awards	• opportunity to develop new and creative approaches that extend or redefine existing knowledge or professional practice • appropriate for leading experts or practitioners in a particular field

The Qualifications and Credit Framework (QCF)

During 2010 the finishing touches will be made to a new way of describing and earning vocational qualifications. Many of the qualifications will stay the same (and many will keep their present name). The new system will make it easier to compare different qualifications and much easier to mix and match different qualifications (or even parts of qualifications) than ever before.

Many vocational qualifications already have a level attached to them. The new system will see a level for every vocational qualification. So it will be much easier to see how each one fits in with all the others.

When you study for a qualification, it will be broken down into units. Each unit is given a level from entry to level 8, as shown on the chart. Qualifications can be made up of units at different levels. The final level of the qualification will depend on the level of the largest group of units.

You are likely to have some choice about which units you do for a particular qualification. Not complete choice, though, as not every school or college can offer every unit.

Each unit carries a specified number of credits. A credit is ten hours of learning. Vocational qualifications will be in three sizes, based on the number of credits.

- Award: 1–12 credits (10 to 120 hours of learning)
- Certificate: 13–36 units (130 to 360 hours of learning)
- Diploma: 37 credits or more (over 370 hours of learning)

But each of these could be at any one of several levels. Here are some examples:

- level 2 Diploma in business skills
- level 3 NVQ in hairdressing
- level 3 Certificate in retail skills
- level 1 Diploma in retail skills.

Every time you earn credits they will be recorded and stored so you can build them up over time. If you have a break in your education QCF credits are not lost. You can start your learning again and continue to earn credits towards a qualification.

When you are making your choices about work-related and work-based learning you do not need to worry too much about this new system. You just need to know that there are changes happening and that some qualifications may have different names from those you have heard before or might be expecting.

Your Connexions personal adviser/careers adviser, teachers and tutors will be able to help you with this. The staff at the colleges, schools or sixth form colleges where you might be thinking of studying will know how to guide you through the new system. Soon it will become familiar to everyone.

National Vocational Qualifications (NVQs)

NVQs are a particular type of vocational qualification. You may have heard of them – some of you may already be working towards them, perhaps at level 1 or possibly level 2. They are workplace qualifications that are designed to test what you know and how well you do your job. This is called 'competency based'.

Instead of taking exams you keep a log showing the tasks you have completed, which is signed off by your supervisor, trainer or NVQ assessor, when they decide you have become competent in a particular area. You also build up a portfolio of evidence, such as assignments or details of particular tasks, that is assessed. People at work are doing NVQs in all sorts of career areas and at different levels, from level 1 right up to level 5, which is aimed at people who have degree-level qualifications, and higher.

As part of the QCF, NVQs are changing too. In some career areas NVQs will start to have new names during 2010 and 2011.

Money matters

Of course it does! The decisions you are making about what to do at 16+ and beyond needn't be based just around money, but you will want to take into account what you are entitled to free, what you might have to pay for and what money you might get coming in.

Do I have to pay for a course?

For the next stage of your education, whether still at school, at sixth-form college or a further education college, you won't have to pay fees.

- If you don't have a level 2 qualification, you will be entitled to free tuition to acquire one at any age, and by any method – full time, part time or through distance learning.

- Anyone aged 19 to 25 will be entitled to free tuition for their first full level 3 qualification (level 3 is A level or equivalent standard).

So, no need to be put off by the thought of fees, if you are thinking of taking further education courses over the next few years.

What about my living costs?

You will need money for your day-to-day living expenses.

Depending on your family's income, you might also be eligible to receive Education Maintenance Allowance (EMA) of up to £30 a week. EMA is available for 16- to 19-year-olds studying full time for one or two years and, in some cases, for three years. You need to be doing at least twelve hours of guided learning per week, on a course up to and including level 3, such as AS/A2, GCSEs or NVQs.

EMA is a weekly payment of £10, £20 or £30 a week during term time, depending on your family's income. The money is meant to help with the day-to-day costs when you stay on at school or college – such as travel, books and equipment. It is paid directly into your bank account (so you'll need to open one if you haven't got one already). If you are entitled to EMA, you'll receive your payment every week of your course in term time as long as you turn up to your classes and show commitment to your course.

It is also possible to earn bonuses of up to £500 over a two-year course. Bonuses depend on the progress you make with your course and are paid at the rate of £100 each January and July, with another £100 in the September just as the second year begins.

So how do you qualify for EMA?

There are some eligibility rules. You will need to:

- be from a household where the income is less than £30,000 a year – check this with your parents or carers

- have your 16th birthday between 1 September and 31 August in the year in which the course starts

- be a UK national born here, or have UK citizenship or a UK passport, have indefinite leave to remain, indefinite leave to enter the UK, or refugee status

or

- come from a European Union or European Economic Area country and have lived in the UK for at least three years and satisfy the home student criteria.

If you are in one of these last groups it is advisable to check your status at www.homeoffice.gov.uk

You can find full information on the EMA website http://moneytolearn.direct.gov.uk.

Other financial help

If you or your family are worried about managing financially, it's worth knowing that colleges have funds to help some students with books and equipment, or the costs of field and study trips and exam fees.

In some areas there is help with fares to school and college for some people.

If you have particular financial need because of special circumstances, such as being on probation or in prison, in the care system or a young parent, there may be extra help available. Ask one of your carers or visit http://moneytolearn.direct.gov.uk.

There may also be help if you are studying a particular course or if you are studying away from home. Again, the above website has details.

Can I work if I go to college or stay on at school?

Yes you can. Most full-time college courses don't keep you in college all day every day. Often there is a day a week when you're not in college or parts of days during the week. So depending on your timetable, you may have time for part-time work.

Not only will this give you a chance to earn some money but you will also be gaining valuable work experience.

If you stay on at school (or go to sixth form college) your hours of attendance will be much the same as you are used to in school. Remember, though, if you are changing from school to college or sixth form college, your journey may be longer, which will cut into your free time.

You may already have a weekend job so there may be nothing to stop you keeping that on when you are 16+.

REMEMBER, though, that most courses expect you to study outside the classroom. If you want to pass the course and get good grades you will need to work on assignments, coursework, essays and projects. And some courses have exams. So don't fill all your time with paid work.

REMEMBER also that EMA (see above) is only paid if you attend your classes – so don't let paid work interfere with this. But the good news is that EMA is NOT affected by your part-time earnings.

So, there is a lot to think about! But you are not on your own. There are people out there to help! Who are they, and what do they do?

People who can help

It's your decision, but you don't have to face the decision making all on your own. There are people who are willing to help you and waiting to help you through this time.

Sometimes it can seem as though there are too many people offering suggestions and advice about what you should do with your life. It can be hard to know who to listen to and whose advice to take.

By now you will probably have started to work out whose views you can trust and who will be the most help to you. Listen to them all – you may be surprised by what good advice you hear.

REMEMBER it's your choice. You're the one who's going to do the course or the job so it's got to feel right for you.

Connexions personal advisers/careers advisers

Their role is to provide free impartial information, advice and guidance to young people and explain the options open to them in their education and training. They can tell you about:

- general or work-related courses and the schools and colleges that offer them
- Apprenticeships
- work and training opportunities
- entry requirements for different careers.

Part of their job involves visiting local employers, so they will be able to tell you which jobs are available, who is recruiting and their entry requirements.

If you decide to stay on in full-time education next year, they can advise you on suitable courses, whether you want to begin building up a set of qualifications that will lead to a particular career or whether you want to keep your options open for the time being.

They can help you to plan ahead and look at degree and Higher Diploma courses, and the entry requirements for different occupations. When it comes to more detailed information on getting a job, they can help you with your application letter or form and tell you how to prepare a CV and how to do well in job interviews.

Connexions personal advisers or Career Wales Youth Gateway advisers can also help you with other aspects of your life, such as problems at home, or health or relationship problems, which may be preventing you from making clear decisions about your future.

Careers teachers/guidance teachers

You will have had careers lessons for some time now, so the members of staff giving them may know you quite well and be able to help you in your decision making. They will also provide assistance with the job application process. You might already have looked at application forms, covering letters, interviews, telephone interviews and so on in careers lessons. You may even have had a chance to role play or do mock interviews.

Personal tutor/form teacher

They won't have the same expert knowledge as the careers specialists, but they will know you better as a person. Don't be afraid to talk choices and decisions over with them too.

Subject teachers

It will be particularly useful, essential in fact, to ask their advice if you are considering taking their subject to a higher level in full-time further education. They will be able to tell you what it will be like studying the subject at a higher level and how it will differ from GCSE work.

Your family

They probably know you better than anyone. You might think that your parents' or carers' information and ideas are out of date – but research shows that the views of parents and carers are important to young people when making career choices. They, and older brothers or sisters, have been through education themselves and may have experience of applying for jobs too. So they can help when you are looking for a job and making applications by looking at your application forms and CVs, and suggesting possible improvements.

Friends

And they also know you! They could be useful sources of advice as to whether you are right for a particular job or employer. Of course they might be just a little too honest...

Information

For factual information, rather than personal advice, there are websites where you can get help. These are good ones to start with:

Connexions Direct www.connexions-direct.com

Careers Wales www.careerswales.com

You can follow the links to services in your area.

Chapter twelve gives more sources of information.

Summary

- All qualification levels relate to each other so you can mix and match.

- Vocational qualifications are changing to units and credits.

- There are lots of sources of help for you to use.

Chapter five

General education?

"It's impressive that you have 228 GCSEs, but it's not enough."

For many careers GCSEs are not enough. As we saw in Chapter three, entrance qualifications are going up. A rapidly changing world of work needs a constant supply of highly trained workers. And once in a job, you will be expected to keep up, or even increase, your skills.

The chapter will cover:

- AS and A levels in general subjects, including Advanced Extension Awards
- Extended Project Qualification
- International Baccalaureate
- Welsh Baccalaureate

- AQA Baccalaureate
- Cambridge Pre-U.

Most of these are designed for university entry but they can be seen as qualifications in their own right and will prepare you for any of the 18+ routes described in Chapter eleven.

AS and A level

AS (or Advanced Subsidiary) level is normally taken in year 12. There is a very large number of subjects to choose from. If you are taking the 100% general academic route, you normally take four subjects – or sometimes more. At the end of year 12 you take AS level exams in all the subjects. In year 13, you continue with two or three of these subjects at A2 level.

However, it isn't necessary to follow this pattern. AS levels are stand-alone qualifications. They do not have to be converted into the full A level. It's possible to stay on for year 13 and take more subjects for AS. But you need to know that most universities require at least two full A levels in their entrance qualifications. Although it is, in theory, possible to make up the required number of points for entry from AS subjects, the leading universities and those offering the more popular courses don't accept this. See the UCAS tariff later in this chapter to see how the different qualifications and grades compare.

Qualifications are so flexible nowadays that, depending on your school or college timetable, you can mix and match them. It's possible to combine general AS and A level subjects with A levels in applied subjects for instance – or with other qualifications. Some examples are given in the case studies in this chapter.

Could you follow the AS/A level route?

There are no fail-safe answers to the question 'Should I follow this more academic path?' but your teachers should have a pretty good idea. They should be able to give you a realistic opinion, but remember, they have to predict outcomes over two years into the future, and changes will occur over that period. When you are considering A levels, bear in mind the following points.

- You need to be sure that you enjoy the subjects you choose and that you are interested enough in them to study them in depth for up to two years.

- If you have a particular career in mind, now is the time to find out which subjects you need and at what level. This may help you decide whether A levels are right for you.

- There are some subjects offered at A level that you will not have met before.

- There are big differences between the study skills required for GCSE and A level. In your GCSEs you are assessed on what you knew, understood and could do, with coursework playing an important part. At A level, though coursework often forms part of the assessment, your grade will largely depend on exams.

- You will need to learn to manage your time. There may be a lot of free time during the school or college day now that you are studying a smaller number of subjects. You will be responsible for deciding how to use your time. You will have to work out how to strike the balance between spending time with your friends, doing the things you want to do and getting the work done.

- For A levels, the teachers are less likely to set pieces of homework that have to be done by the next lesson. They are more likely to suggest that you do some reading or research. You will need to be much more self-motivated than for GCSEs and take more responsibility for your own learning and independent study – good skills to acquire before going into either higher education or employment.

Entry requirements to AS and A level courses

Each school and college is free to set its own standard. The generally accepted minimum, however, is four GCSE passes at A*-C, usually in the subjects you want to do at A level. Some schools and colleges will ask for five, and some A level subjects may have a higher level requirement – grade B, perhaps.

What will A and AS levels give me?

You might find yourself asking 'Why would any employer want my knowledge of history or English literature?' In some jobs the subject matter of the A level is important – if you want to teach, for example, or go into scientific laboratory work. But the wider value of academic A level study is in the transferable skills you will acquire.

By the end of an A level course you will have learned how to:

- assimilate new information
- bring together information from different sources
- decide which information is relevant
- summarise arguments
- communicate
- present a reasoned argument
- analyse information critically
- structure an essay or report
- think for yourself
- weigh up evidence and opposing arguments
- reach conclusions and solutions
- manage your own study.

Quite an impressive list – and one that many employers will see the value of.

A levels, regardless of subject, demonstrate that you are capable of following further study and training.

For and against

Not all 16+ routes are suitable for everyone. There are advantages and disadvantages to each one. Here are some arguments FOR and AGAINST studying general AS and A levels.

For

- Some careers have academic entry requirements. Most professions, for example, ask for a degree. It is possible to go to university with other level 3 qualifications (BTEC National or NVQ level 3, for example) but A levels show that you can deal with an academic course.

- GCSEs on their own will not be enough to get you into university.

- In many careers you will be expected to study further for professional qualifications. A level study is a good preparation.

- If you decide to go into employment at 18+ you will probably interview better than younger applicants and you may find that A levels give you a higher salary than those who entered the same business at 16.

- A level study can be a very satisfying experience, classes are smaller and there is usually a closer relationship between teachers and students. Teaching becomes much less formal. Most students find that they are treated as young adults rather than school pupils.

- You will be able to study a few subjects that you really enjoy, knowing that you are progressing towards the career you have chosen.

And against

- You may feel that five years of secondary education is enough and you are ready for something different.

- You may already know what career area you are interested in and have a clear idea of the usual entry routes and levels. (Chapter ten has more on this.)

- Some jobs are easier to enter with vocational qualifications (see Chapter six) especially if you have a clear idea of what you want to do.

- Some careers, such as agriculture or horticulture, require practical experience before you start in them. A levels alone will not provide this. You would have to take advice as to which age would be most appropriate to enter these career areas.

- Although you want to study at A level, you want to include some work-related learning. Applied A levels may be the course for you, either with other vocational courses or with general academic A levels (Chapter six has more on applied A levels).

Which subjects can you take at AS and A level?

There are around 80 different A level subjects accredited by the Qualifications and Curriculum Authority (QCA). The detail of the content varies with the different exam boards and they will not all be available in every single school or college. Generally speaking, the larger the school or college the wider the choice of subjects.

You might be able to choose from:

accounting
ancient history
Arabic
anthropology
archaeology
art and design
art history
biblical Hebrew
biology
business studies
chemistry
Chinese
citizenship studies
classical civilisation
communication studies
computing and IT
critical thinking
dance
design and technology – product design
design and technology – systems and control
design and technology – textiles
drama and theatre studies
economics
economics and business
electronics
English language
English language and literature
English literature
environmental studies/science
food technology

French
film studies
general studies
geography
geology
German
government and politics
Greek (classical)
Gujarati
history
history of art
home economics
human biology
ICT
Italian
Japanese
Latin
law
mathematics (and further mathematics)
mathematics (pure and discrete)
mathematics (pure and mechanics)
mathematics (pure and statistical)
media studies
modern Hebrew
music
music technology
Panjabi
Persian
philosophy
physical education/sports studies

physics

Polish

Portuguese

psychology

religious studies

Russian

science in society

social policy

sociology

Spanish

theology

Turkish

Urdu

use of mathematics

Welsh

There are also a few AS levels that do not lead on to the full A level, such as science for public understanding.

The shape of the AS/A level course

An AS is worth half an A level and consists of two or three units. It covers the less demanding material in the A level course and is assessed at the standard expected halfway through an A level course.

If you go on to A2 in any or all of your AS subjects, you will study two or three more units. They will cover the AS topics in more depth and introduce new topics.

How are the courses assessed?

- Usually, you study a module or unit and then sit the exam. Schools do have the option to set all the exams at the end of the course and some do so.

- Most modular schemes offer a good degree of flexibility and allow you to either 'cash in' modular grades to obtain an AS pass or carry on to A2 to gain the full A level.

- You may re-sit each unit once in order to improve a particular grade.

- Coursework also has a place and can count for between 20% and 30% of the final mark. Some subjects, for example critical thinking, contain no coursework and all assessment is by examination.

- You would also do some, if not all, end-of-course exams in the summer.

- One of the exams for a full A level will be a synoptic paper, which covers elements of all units. The marks for this paper will make up 20% of the full A level award.

When everything has been marked and added together, you are given a grade from A* to E. (A* grades are awarded from summer 2010 for A2).

What is A level like?

Like GCSEs, A levels are single subject exams. Remember that:

- most people take four subjects at AS and three at A2
- a few take more
- taking two is still worthwhile
- studying just one may limit your options for higher education – it is possible to begin a Higher National Diploma or foundation degree course with just one A level but some courses ask for other qualifications alongside.

By taking two or three subjects you are starting to specialise. In theory you can combine any subjects but REMEMBER:

- some combinations may not be possible in some schools and colleges because of timetabling
- some combinations may limit your options later on – you may need to check with your personal adviser/careers adviser, because some combinations are more useful than others, especially if you have a particular career in mind.

Most people find the work at A level much more demanding than at GCSE. In some subjects there is a greater emphasis on writing essays than previously and, certainly, A level is more theoretically based. Many people would argue that there is a greater difference between GCSE and A level than between A level and university study. If you have GCSEs at grades A*-C in a good breadth of subjects, however, you should be able to cope.

How do I choose my AS and A levels?

There are a number of points from which you start to answer a question like this. Take first the careers reference point. By the time you get to year 11, you might:

- know your career intentions
- have only a general career idea
- still be waiting for a career plan to emerge.

What steps should you take in each of these cases?

If you know which career interests you

If you have made up your mind about a future career and discussed this with others, including your careers teacher, personal adviser/ careers adviser, subject teachers, parents or carers and other interested people, then you will know what the entry requirements are in terms of examination passes and whether the career involves further education or on-the-job training.

This will give you a target to aim at while you are at school, which might be A levels, AS, GCSEs or any combination of these. You will have a good idea, after taking exams in year 11 and discussing the results with teaching staff, where your subject strengths and weaknesses lie. This should help you with your subject choice for the next two years. So, if you can clearly see your career destination, find out the subject requirements for it and build a well-balanced programme around them.

If you have a general career idea

If you have broadly chosen your career field, but are not certain exactly which career you would like to aim at, then you will want to get all the help and advice you can and keep your options open. But remember, your advisers can only give information, advice and guidance – you make the final choice. Perhaps you will decide to leave the career decision open by looking at a broad group of careers – such as creative careers or engineering. If this is so, then you can begin to think about entry levels. Will you want to begin training for a career at 18 or after a degree? There is more help with this in Chapter ten.

You can certainly make some plans now – but you will not be committed. There is more than one route to many jobs. There is scope for changing your mind.

According to the structure of the career, and with advice from the careers staff, you can pinpoint the subjects you will need. If you have decided on the 18+ entry, for example, you may discover that the career group you have chosen requires a high ability in maths. Your subject teachers will soon tell you whether they think you might reach a satisfactory standard at A level. You will then know whether your target is realistic. It's all a matter of balancing what you want against what is required of you.

If you have no career plan at all

Then don't worry too much. Try to keep your options open. This still means getting careers information, advice and guidance – if only so that you know which careers would not be possible if you stopped studying certain subjects. In other words, knowing what you don't want to do in the future could be just as important at this stage as having a career plan all mapped out!

So, consider the subjects you enjoy doing and, usually closely related to this, those you are good at. If you have a broad base of GCSE grades at C or above and, for example, enjoy a science subject such as physics and have achieved a fair measure of success in it, then this would clearly be a natural choice for A level. As a full A level programme usually involves following three subjects, you should now consider which others would be the most appropriate to take with physics – one other could be a science or maths subject, but the third could be a humanities subject or a foreign language. This will keep as many doors open as possible, which is the best idea for anyone who has no definite career in mind.

James is studying physics, maths and food technology at A2 in year 13. Last year he studied these subjects at AS along with chemistry

---

'I know I want to go to university to study civil engineering so an academic course was my first choice. I wanted to get a good grounding in maths and physics and decided to combine them with chemistry for A2. I did well in my GCSEs so most of my teachers were happy for me to take the A level. In some ways that made it harder to choose so I decided to go for an AS subject that I enjoy. I love cooking and I'm interested in nutrition, particularly how it affects my fitness for sports. My school is a specialist technology college and the facilities for food tech are excellent.

I'm glad I chose food tech as I found chemistry much harder than I expected. My AS result wasn't as good as predicted so I had to think hard over the summer. In the end, after discussing it at home and at school, I decided to take food tech at A2 instead of chemistry. It was a difficult decision but I'm hoping that this will give me the results I need for my university offers.'

You can also look at subject choice from the learning point of view. Think about your preferred study methods and ask yourself the following questions.

- Do my subjects form a sensible pattern?
- Does the course involve a problem-solving approach?
- How appealing is a new subject I haven't studied before?
- How important will written English be?
- How much factual learning will be involved?
- Is there any overlap between the subject areas I am considering?
- Is wide reading necessary?
- Is year 11 success a good predictor in my case?
- What kinds of skills does each subject demand?
- Will there be any practical work in the examination?

Jay looked forward to pursuing his academic interests in the sixth form

---

'I enjoy studying, but only the subjects I like! I found having to do so many subjects at GCSE a bit frustrating as I had to spend time on the ones I don't really enjoy which meant less time to spend on history, for example. I knew I wanted to go to uni, probably to do history, but didn't know what I wanted to do after that. I decided to do all my favourite subjects in the sixth form – also the subjects I'm best at – English, history and maths, with religious studies AS. I loved doing all the reading and turning that into essays but I also like the contrast of the logical challenge of maths.'

What would you study on a course?

Obviously you need to know what is going to be involved! Many schools and colleges produce short leaflets outlining the topics to be covered, the likely workload, teaching methods and the assessment (essays, projects, exams, etc).

You can also find out a good deal by asking subject teachers – either at your own school or at the place you are thinking of attending. Most hold open evenings where you can talk to teachers and often students as well. You can also ask friends a year ahead of you who are already doing the work.

Sample AS and A level programmes

AS/A2 English language and literature

In each unit, students are expected to read widely from a suggested list and from their own research. This can include films, plays and broadcasts as well as travel writing, political texts, obituaries, online content and newspaper features.

Year 1 (AS)

Unit 1: Exploring voices in speech and writing

Students will explore spoken and written language from 20th and 21st century texts to learn how written voices are created and spoken voices are used. One prose text is studied closely but students also use a range of poetry, prose and drama from different sources, including broadcasts, transcripts and electronic communications.

There is one exam where students will analyse short unseen passages as well as answering questions on the set text that they have studied (using a clean copy of the text).

Unit 2: Creating texts

Students develop their own skills as writers for different purposes and different audiences. To inform their writing they study one prose fiction text (different from Unit 1) and another text – either drama or poetry.

Students produce a coursework folder of writing, within strict word limits, on a specified topic. Pieces are for a range of audiences, both reading and listening as well as a commentary on their writing process.

Year 2 (A2)

Unit 3: Varieties in language and literature

Students apply the skills and knowledge of literary and linguistic concepts and approaches that they gained from the AS units. They study either two drama or two poetry texts. At this stage students are expected to make connections between texts and work more independently.

In the exam students are presented with an unseen prose non-fiction extract as well as answering questions on the texts they have studied (again using clean copies).

Unit 4: Presenting the world

This unit focuses on the presentation of the human experience through the study of a range of writers in English. Students are expected to build on their earlier studies.

Students produce a folder of their own literary and non-fiction writing for a defined purpose and audience. Again, this is to a strict word limit and includes an analytical evaluative commentary. Some may be group tasks.

AS/A2 ICT

Year 1 (AS)

Unit 1: Information, systems and applications

Covers the basis concepts of ICT:

- data, information, knowledge and processing
- software and hardware components of an information system
- characteristics of standard applications software and application areas
- spreadsheet concepts
- relational database concepts
- applications software used for presentation and communication of data
- the role and impact of ICT.

There is one exam with long- and short-answer questions.

Unit 2: Structured ICT tasks

Students undertake specified tasks covering practical aspects of ICT, including:

- design
- software development
- testing
- documentation.

Year 2 (A2)

Unit 3: ICT systems, applications and implications

Covers communications between computers and interactions between humans and computers and the impact of ICT on society, commerce and industry:

- the systems cycle
- designing computer-based information systems
- networks and communications
- applications of ICT
- implementing computer-based information systems
- implications of ICT.

There is one exam and students have to answer all questions.

Unit 4: ICT project

This allows students to develop their skills, knowledge and understanding. The project requires analysis of a client-driven problem and design of a solution which is evaluated and presented in a report.

New subjects

It is possible to study many A level subjects without having done the GCSE course – in some cases there is no GCSE course in that subject.

Some of the subjects you may study without doing the GCSE first include:

accounting

archaeology

art and design

art history

business studies

classical civilisation

communication studies

dance

design and technology

drama and theatre studies

economics

electronics

environmental studies/science

film studies

fine art

food technology

general studies

geology

government and politics

human biology

law

media studies

some modern languages such as Russian, Chinese, Spanish

music technology

philosophy

politics

psychology

religious studies/theology

sociology

Sami decided to take psychology A level even though she had not studied the subject before

'It felt like a bit of a gamble, taking a new subject. I know I want to do something health- or medical-related and it seemed like an ideal subject. But how would I know what it's like? Would I like the course? I talked to some year 12s who were doing it. The more I heard about it, the better it sounded. I'm glad I took the risk. Some of the topics are really interesting. At the moment we're looking at how CBT (cognitive behavioural therapy) is used and whether it has worked. We have to look at the published evidence. We're expected to do a lot of our own research, I find it so interesting that I spend ages looking it up on the internet.'

A and AS levels are offered by one of several examination boards. Your school or college will decide which one to use. They are:

- AQA – Assessment and Qualifications Alliance
- Edexcel
- OCR – Oxford, Cambridge and RSA Examinations
- WJEC/CBAC – Welsh Joint Education Committee/Cyd-bwyllgor Addsyg Cymru.

These boards also offer a wide range of vocational qualifications, which are covered in Chapter six.

Advanced Extension Award

This is available in maths to test the most able students by encouraging them to think beyond what they have been taught. There is an extra three-hour exam with grades awarded of distinction or merit.

Extended Project Qualification

You would do this alongside your other year 12 and 13 courses and it is designed to stretch the most able students. It is a single piece of work similar in size to an AS level (or half an A level). You can use it to link together elements from different AS/A levels or to study a particular topic in more depth (this could be from a school subject or something related to an outside interest).

It attracts UCAS points for university entry – more on this later in the chapter. It can be an excellent preparation for university as it uses many of the skills needed on higher education courses, such as investigative research and independent learning.

Assessment

The Extended Project is graded A*-E and could take the form of a design, a report, a dissertation, a piece of art or design that you have created, or a performance (or a combination of these).

The International Baccalaureate

The International Baccalaureate (IB) originated in French speaking countries.

The IB has been around for some time – it is taught in nearly 3,000 schools in over 130 countries around the world. It is not available in all schools in the UK – there are around 150 schools and colleges that offer it, so if you think you'd like to study it you will need to find out if there is a centre nearby. The International Baccalaureate Schools and Colleges Association website www.ibsca.org.uk has a list.

The aim of the IB is to provide a broad and balanced, but academically demanding, course that develops skills in:

- analysing and presenting information
- evaluating and constructing arguments
- solving problems creatively.

The IB encourages an international outlook and intercultural skills.

The qualification offered is the IB Diploma. Students choose one subject from each of six different subject groups:

- literature in your own language
- a second language (either a new one or one you have studied before, including classical languages)
- individuals and societies (geography, history, psychology, business, economics, history, IT)
- experimental sciences (biology, chemistry, design technology, physics)
- mathematics and computer science
- the arts (film, music, theatre, visual arts).

Normally three subjects are studied at higher level and three at standard level.

The core has three parts:

- extended essay – up to 4,000 words, on a topic of individual interest, developing independent research and writing skills
- theory of knowledge and creativity – reflecting critically on the role and nature of knowledge in your own and other cultures
- creativity, action, service – a programme of community service, music, theatre or sports activity.

All are compulsory. In some schools and colleges subjects other than the languages may be a taught in French or Spanish as well as in English.

Assessment

There is a mix of assessment methods.

- Externally marked exams are the basis. Exam questions can take different forms such as essays, multiple choice, structured problems and short response questions.
- Teacher assessments can include oral language work, geography field work, laboratory work and artistic performances.
- Externally assessed work varies from 20% to 50% of the total mark, with a higher percentage in music, theatre and visual arts. The theory of knowledge and extended essays are marked externally.

The top grades are above A level A* grades.

Gabi is in year 12. She decided to take the IB Diploma in the sixth form rather than A levels

'My school offers the IB as well as A levels but we have to choose one or the other – it's not possible to combine the two. We are on a completely different timetable from the A level classes. I have to do six subjects for the IB, which is one of the reasons why I chose it. There were so many subjects I enjoyed and didn't want to give up. I like the variety of the six, rather than concentrating on three or four. It feels much broader. I chose English, history and physics at standard level and maths, Latin and classical Greek, and art at *higher level. I like the teaching style, too. Our classes are small – up to ten – so we can spend a lot of time having discussions – it's such a good way to learn. This was another of the attractions of the IB. I seem to be learning to think in a different way, more globally, I suppose, and to put it into context. It's definitely not an easy option. We have about 18 hours of homework a week across all the subjects. The deadlines are usually around three days, or two weeks for bigger assignments, so I have to organise my time carefully.'*

The Welsh Baccalaureate

The Welsh Baccalaureate is completely different from the International Baccalaureate (which is offered in several school in Wales, see www.ibsca.org.uk).

It combines existing qualifications, such as A levels, NVQs and GCSEs, with personal development. It is taught in English, Welsh or a combination of the two and is available in every local authority area in Wales.

Study is at three levels.

Level	Equivalent to
Foundation	GCSE grades D-G NVQ level 1 Principal Learning Level 1
Intermediate	GCSE grades A*-C NVQ level 2
Advanced	A levels NVQ level 3

There are two parts – core and options. The options element is chosen from existing qualifications at an appropriate level, which could be GCSEs, A levels, BTEC, Principal Learning or project. The core programme components are:

- key skills

- Wales, Europe and the world – can include a language module

- work-related education – working with an employer and a team enterprise activity

- personal and social education – issues in the modern world including an activity in the community
- individual investigation – a research project into an area of interest.

By 2011, Principal Learning will be offered in 14 different occupational areas.

Assessment

There is no assessment of the Welsh Baccalaureate over and above the exams for the options elements. Students compile evidence of their competence in the key skills, which is assessed by their teachers, and present an individual investigation on an aspect of the core learning.

AQA Baccalaureate

This is available to students studying at least 3 A levels and is intended to add value to sixth form qualifications to give students an edge when applying for 18+ options such as jobs, university or Advanced Apprenticeships. It is currently (2010) available in around 250 schools in England.

The AQA Baccalaureate (AQA Bacc) is an addition to the courses students are already taking in years 12 and 13 (usually AS/A levels or an Advanced Diploma). There are three elements.

- Broader study – an AS level in citizenship, critical thinking or general studies.

- Enrichment activities – 100 hours spent in or out of school. Activities must be across at least two of work-related learning, community participation or personal development. Examples include paid employment, young enterprise, work shadowing, leadership roles in school or elsewhere, or representing the school in sports or in public speaking.

- Extended project – a further exploration of a subject you are already studying or a topic of personal interest as described above.

Assessment

The broader study is assessed by the usual methods for the relevant AS. You have to get an E grade or above for it to contribute to the AQA Bacc.

For enrichment activities you keep a personal development log.

Cambridge Pre-U

This is intended to prepare students for university entry by developing the study skills that they will need for higher education. It calls for independent, self-directed learning. It is a two-year course for years 12 and 13. The subjects can be taken separately or combined for a diploma. It is currently (2010) available in around 100 schools in the UK.

Study consists of:

- principal subjects – three chosen from a list of twenty-six
- global perspectives – one chosen from ethics, economics, environment technology, or politics and culture
- independent research report.

Topics are studied for the whole two years, unlike the modular format of AS/A levels.

It is also possible to take one or two A levels as principal subjects.

Assessment

This is by exams at the end of the two years. The five subjects are graded separately as either distinction, merit or pass. The top grade is above A level A* grade (and above the top grade for the International Baccalaureate).

Combining different qualifications

Chapter four showed you that many young people choose to combine academic, general courses with work-related qualifications, and showed you some examples. There is more about work-related qualifications in Chapter six.

You may choose to combine different academic qualifications from this chapter – and you may want (or need) to retake some GCSEs. The possibilities will depend on the school or sixth form college where you study.

What are my results worth?

University admissions are organised through UCAS. You will hear of offers of places in higher education being made on the basis of UCAS points. These are calculated by allocating numerical scores to the grades you achieve.

The UCAS tariff

The tariff is designed to equate all the different kinds of advanced qualifications. However, university admissions tutors can decide themselves how many points they ask for, for a particular course. They can also decide which qualifications they are prepared to accept. So the top universities will only accept points from A levels, especially for the most popular courses. Others might ask for 360 points with at least two A levels at grade A (with additional points from a third A level plus other qualifications). Each university and college is different, and sometimes it differs from course to course. So it's very important to check carefully on the UCAS website and on the universities' and colleges' own websites.

Here are some examples of UCAS points.

Grade	Applied A level (single award)	A level	AS
A* (from 2010)	140	140	
A	120	120	60
B	100	100	50
C	80	80	40
D	60	60	30
E	40	40	20

Applied A level double award

Grade A*A*	280 (from 2010)
Grade A*A	260 (from 2010)
Grade AA	240 points
Grade AB	220 points
Grade BB	200 points
Grade BC	180 points
Grade CC	160 points
Grade CD	140 points
Grade DD	120 points
Grade DE	100 points
Grade EE	80 points

IB Diploma	280 to 720 points, depending on level achieved
Welsh Baccalaureate Core	120 points (within the Advanced Diploma)
Extended Project	20 to 70 points, depending on grades
Cambridge Pre-U	20 to 145 points for each element, depending on grades

Other qualifications such as Grades 6, 7 and 8 music exams and ASDAN Community Volunteering also carry points.

The tariff is updated as new qualifications are added. You can see it on the UCAS website: www.ucas.com.

Summary

- Think carefully about whether academic study is right for you.
- Not all subjects and options are available at all schools and colleges.
- There are academic alternatives to AS and A levels.

Chapter six

Work-related education?

This chapter looks at the route of remaining in full-time education, and taking a career-related course (see the chart in Chapter four).

As the name suggests work-related qualifications, also called vocational qualifications, train you for the world of work. Some of them are very specialised and train you for one job or career area only. Others are more broadly based and start training you for a wide occupational area, such as business, or art and design.

The specialised qualifications are obviously ideal for people who have a clear idea of the job they want to do. They can start straightaway on their education and training for their career. For example, if you know that you want to work with children it might suit you to start working towards qualifications for a career in early years.

However, if you have not yet decided exactly what you want to do but have an idea of which occupational area you want to end up in, then a broad-based vocational course may be right for you. Perhaps you know, for example, that you want to work in health and social care, but you haven't yet decided which aspect of it you would prefer. A health and social care course would give you a chance to study the elderly, children, nursing care and mental health, and to specialise later.

Many vocational courses, both specialised and broad based, include visits to employers or even work placements, which can be a really good way to help you decide which is the right career for you. If you already know which career you want to follow, then a work placement gives you valuable experience.

Because all qualifications nowadays are part of the National Qualifications Framework (see Chapter four), vocational courses are equivalent to the general academic GCSE and A level qualifications. Vocational qualifications also carry UCAS points.

But you do need to REMEMBER that universities set their own entrance requirements, and some may prefer academic rather than vocational qualifications.

The work-related (vocational) courses include:

- applied A levels
- BTEC Nationals
- OCR Nationals
- NVQs
- Diplomas (England only)
- applied GCSEs and other level 2 courses
- Foundation Learning and Entry to Employment (e2e)
- Skill Build (Wales).

Where can I study?

Vocational courses are offered by:

- school sixth forms – either your own or one nearby
- sixth form colleges
- colleges of further education.

Again not all choices are available in all areas. Not all schools have sixth forms, so in this case you will have to move somewhere else to study beyond 16.

Sometimes it's possible to stay based at your present school and study subjects offered at other places – another sixth form perhaps. If you opt for one of the new Diploma courses (available in England) you are likely to do at least part of your study in another place.

There is more on the differences between schools and colleges in Chapter eight.

Here are some of the arguments FOR and AGAINST work-related education.

For

- Taking career-related qualifications can give you a more varied 16+ programme of study. (You can mix and match with GCSEs and general AS and A levels if you wish.)

- In their own right, they are qualifications that will take you into employment and higher education.

- They are relevant to particular employment sectors and can be a good introduction to the world of work.

- The courses have a practical, investigative approach to learning. You will be finding things out by trying them out for yourself.

- Although you will work on set topics, you have a lot of control over how you plan and go about your work.

- Your course will take you out of school or college – for example on visits or on work experience placements.

- Work-related courses can be very job specific or they can be in a broad area, so they need not tie you down to a particular job.

- They can help you with your career choices – you might get some ideas on possible careers or find out about jobs that you did not know existed. You might hit on exactly the career you want to follow.

And against

- Some students worry that such qualifications may not be recognised by higher education admissions tutors. (This is dealt with later in this chapter.)

- Mixing and matching flexibly can't always be done. Although schools and colleges are as flexible as they can be in offering everyone their choice of subjects, timetabling can make some choices impossible. You can't be in two places at the same time!

- Not every school or college can offer every course.

- Students also worry that some employers might think the work-related education route is a soft option. It isn't. It's hard work.

Advanced (level 3) qualifications

If you want to study at this level you will have to get used to new ways of working. There will be a big difference between working for these qualifications and doing GCSEs.

- You will find that you are expected to take more responsibility for your own learning and do a lot more independent research and study than you have done before. (This is a good skill to acquire before going into either higher education or employment.)

- You will need to learn to manage your time. You will be given a lot of assignments and investigations to do – often by several teachers at the same time! It will be up to you to decide when to do each of them and to plan a work timetable for yourself so that you are not always in a last minute rush.

- Some projects and assignments are likely to be set as group exercises. This means that you will be working with other people – and you all have to make sure that everyone pulls their weight. Nobody likes the person who leaves most of the work on a joint project to other people but tries to share in the credit. (This happens at work too, so if it happens to you it will be good experience.)

Applied A levels

These are very broad based work-related courses. You would not leave school or college fully qualified and trained for a job after doing the course. The courses are designed to develop the knowledge and skills needed for jobs in a broad field of work. So, on completing an A level in an applied subject, you would have a very good introduction to a career area and you should have gained relevant work experience.

A levels in applied subjects could lead you to:

- employment
- an Apprenticeship
- higher education.

They are available in:

- applied science
- art and design
- business
- engineering
- health and social care
- ICT
- leisure studies
- media
- performing arts
- travel and tourism.

Some of these subjects are also offered as general A levels. What is the difference? The A level in an applied subject is more work related. In art and design, for instance, if you chose the general A level your work would be more personally creative. If you chose the applied one you would be more likely to have assignments asking you to respond to a client's brief for a project. It will pay to compare both courses carefully and ask questions. To help you see the difference, Chapter five has an outline of A level ICT and later in this chapter there is an outline of the applied A level in ICT.

In applied A levels much of the work is based around projects and investigation. Courses are likely to include visits to relevant organisations and lectures by guest speakers.

A lot of the assessment is based on your coursework. It is graded in exactly the same way as general A levels, with pass grades of A*-E.

You can take one of four main qualifications:

- AS level – three AS units, graded A-E
- AS level (double award) – six AS units graded AA, AB, BB, BC, CC, CD, DD, DE or EE
- A level – six units (three AS units and three A2 units) graded A*-E
- A level (double award) – 12 units (six AS units and six A level units) graded A*A*, A*A, AA, AB, BB, BC, CC, CD, DD, DE or EE.

A* grades are awarded from summer 2010 for A2.

(Not all applied subjects are available as double awards.)

In Wales, WJEC/CBAC qualifications have four units for the single award A level and eight units for the double award A level. WJEC/CBAC applied science has single awards only.

Entry requirements to applied AS and A level courses

Each school and college is free to set its own standard. The usual minimum, however, is four GCSE passes at A*-C. To study some subjects at some schools and colleges you might be asked for GCSE passes in particular subjects. You might also sometimes be asked for B grades. Alternative level 2 qualifications may be accepted.

What does each area cover?

Applied science

Compared with single subject sciences this course takes an integrated approach to science and emphasises the application of scientific principles. You will learn how science has developed and the impact on present-day society. The course also covers the importance of science as a human activity and how it relates to the social, philosophical, environmental and industrial aspects of the world. You will have a chance to study in greater depth some aspects of science including sports, pathology, the environment, medicine or the body.

Art and design

The course is aimed at developing art and design skills through working on design briefs. You will gain experience of a wide range of 2D and 3D techniques and associated equipment. You will develop the skills, knowledge and understanding that artists, craftspeople and designers need to create their work. By studying the work practices of individuals and small businesses you will learn how meaning is created and communicated. You will be encouraged to experiment with media and materials.

Business

The course develops an understanding of how business works in the real world. You will study aspects of business such as human resources, marketing and finance, and how these relate to businesses as a whole. By taking part in an enterprise activity, you will discover the problems and opportunities faced by businesses. Other practical activities might include planning and building a website or organising an event.

Engineering

The course aims to give an understanding of the processes and skills needed when working in engineering. It also addresses the wider issues regarding the role of engineering and technology in society and its relationship with the environment. You will study engineering processes and techniques, the role of the engineer and principles of design and prototyping. You will also study materials and basic engineering maths.

Health and social care

The course aims to help you develop the skills needed for the health and social care sector, including research, evaluation and problem solving. You will have the chance to apply your learning to different care contexts such as health, children's services and older people. You will study promoting health and wellbeing, disease, lifestyle choices, communication and values, and human growth and development.

ICT

Through this course you will develop an understanding of the main principles of problem solving using IT. The course will encourage you to keep up with developments in ICT. You will also gain an understanding of the wider environment in which ICT is used, by studying e-business, digital marketing and project planning.

Leisure studies

You will study the wide range of activities forming the leisure industry, including home-based leisure, sport, countryside, lifelong learning and heritage. The course looks at leisure customers, leisure organisations and current developments in leisure, including the use of technology. You will learn about the law relating to the industry and the business systems and models involved.

Media

The course will help you develop skills and knowledge relevant to the particular sector, while giving you an overview of the structure of the industry, including digital, print, TV and film. As well as gaining an understanding of professional practice, you will have a chance to showcase this in a show reel or portfolio. The course encourages independence and self-directed learning. You will develop media-related skills relevant to a client-orientated context.

Performing arts

You will be encouraged to develop your performance or production skills by putting on a performance for an external examiner. You will learn how a performance is realised, taking in both creative and organisational aspects. In addition, the course will give you an insight into the performing arts industry and the issues facing it, together with a knowledge of the working methods used by arts professionals as individuals, in teams and with audiences.

Travel and tourism

As well as learning practical and technical skills relevant to the travel and tourism industries, you will have an opportunity for in-depth study of one or more sectors. You will also learn how the different sectors interact and inter-relate. At the end of the course you will have an appreciation of the diversity and complexity of the travel and tourism industry and some of the issues facing it. The course includes UK and European tourism, resort operations, promotion and sales, travelling safely and special interest holidays.

Applied A level programme

Applied ICT (single award)

Year 1 (AS)

Unit 1: Using ICT to communicate

- the information age
- communication of information
- accuracy and readability
- styles of presentation
- how organisations present information
- standard ways of working

Students create a portfolio.

Unit 2: How organisations use ICT

- types of organisation
- functions within organisations
- information and its use
- ICT systems
- the impact of ICT on working practices
- the impact of ICT on methods of production
- legislation

There is one exam.

Unit 3: ICT solutions for individuals and society

- public service websites
- search engines
- databases
- use of spreadsheet facilities
- development of spreadsheets to present results of data analysis
- presentation of the results of an investigation

Students prepare a portfolio.

Year 2 (A2)

Unit 4: Working to a brief

- understand a set brief and plan to meet its requirements
- identification of skills
- work with others
- plan, develop and deliver a project
- evaluate

Students are assessed on the project task.

Unit 5: Numerical modelling using spreadsheets

- develop a working specification
- design and development of spreadsheets
- implement a spreadsheet solution
- present spreadsheet information
- test and document the development
- evaluate

Students prepare a portfolio.

Unit 6: Interactive multimedia products

- review multimedia products
- consider design
- design and create an interactive multimedia product
- test and document product
- evaluate

Students produce a portfolio.

Mike is taking applied science A level. He is in year 12

'I chose the double award in applied science because it covers all three sciences and gives me two A levels. There's a big workload, though! For me it's more interesting looking at the sciences together rather than studying them separately. And we're constantly looking at how science fits into the real world. When we were looking at how different fuels burn, we had to assess the applications and

limitations of each one. We also did a risk assessment of the whole exercise. Sport's my other big interest so I'm really enjoying the unit on science in sport.'

Other level 3 qualifications

Many schools or colleges offer **either** BTEC **or** OCR programmes in any particular subject. So you will need to look carefully to see which might suit you better.

OCR Nationals at level 3

These are still level 3 qualifications, but most of them are more specialised than applied A levels and relate to specific occupational areas. You can take OCR Nationals in:

- art and design
- business
- health, social care and early years
- ICT
- media
- public services
- sport
- travel and tourism.

There are three qualifications, each requiring a different number of mandatory units (which you have to do) and optional units (which you can choose):

- Certificate – four mandatory and two optional units
- Diploma – four mandatory and eight optional units
- Extended Diploma – four mandatory and fourteen optional units.

Within each subject area there are specialist pathways.

Sample programme

(Please note, however, that under the Qualifications and Credit Framework (QCF) being developed in 2010, the structure and content of courses may be changing.)

OCR level 3 National in business

Mandatory units:

- investigating business
- customer service
- business communications
- finance for business.

Optional non-specialist units:

- marketing for business
- practical sales skills
- law in the business world
- working in international business
- career planning for business
- work experience in business.

Optional units – enterprise specialist pathway:

- research, innovation, design and development
- skills and the entrepreneur
- e-marketing
- e-business.

Optional units – personnel and management specialist pathway:

- human resource management
- strategic management
- recruitment and selection
- training and development
- employee relations
- motivating and empowering people.

Optional units – business systems specialist pathway:

- practical administration
- quality systems
- production
- distribution.

There are no formal exams. Assessment is by the most appropriate method. For example, assessment of a multimedia product would be by looking at the html files (rather than by looking at hard copies of files).

All units are graded pass, merit or distinction, giving an overall award for the qualification.

Points are given equivalents on the UCAS tariff (see Chapter five for an explanation of the tariff).

The National Diploma is equivalent to two A levels. The Extended Diploma is equivalent to three A levels, or an A level plus a double award applied A level.

There is more information about OCR Nationals on the OCR website www.ocrnational.com.

BTEC National qualifications

These have been designed in consultation with employers to meet the needs of the different occupational areas. There is a wide range of subjects:

- aerospace engineering
- agriculture
- animal management
- applied law
- applied science
- art and design
- aviation operations
- beauty therapy sciences
- blacksmithing and metalworking
- business
- central and local government
- children's care, learning and development
- communications technology
- construction, building services engineering and civil engineering

- countryside management
- dental technology
- electrical/electronic engineering
- engineering
- fish management
- floristry
- forestry and arboriculture
- hairdressing
- health and social care
- horse management
- horticulture
- hospitality
- IT practitioners
- land-based technology
- manufacturing engineering
- mechanical engineering
- media
- music and music technology
- operations and maintenance engineering
- performing arts
- personal and business finance
- pharmacy services
- polymer processing and materials technology
- production arts
- retail
- sport
- sport and exercise sciences
- travel and tourism

- uniformed public services
- vehicle technology.

Within each subject there is a range of level 3 qualifications, for example in construction and the built environment:

- Certificate in construction and the built environment
- Subsidiary Diploma in construction and the built environment
- Diploma in construction and the built environment
- Extended Diploma in construction and the built environment
- Diploma in construction and the built environment (civil engineering)
- Extended Diploma in construction and the built environment (civil engineering)
- Diploma in construction and the built environment (building services engineering)
- Extended Diploma in construction and the built environment (building services engineering).

Again, these are designed to meet the needs of different sectors of the construction industry.

Entry requirements are usually four GCSEs (A*-C) or a BTEC First qualification. Other level 2 qualifications may also be accepted.

Each qualification has either mandatory units (which you have to study), or optional units (which you choose from) or a mixture of the two. Each unit carries a number of credits, which add up to make the qualification. Each qualification requires a different number of credits:

- Certificate – 30 credits
- Subsidiary Diploma – 60 credits
- Diploma – 120 credits
- Extended Diploma – 180 credits.

There are no exams – units are assessed on an ongoing basis against a set of outcomes. You will have to complete a variety of coursework including portfolios, case studies, presentations and practical projects. You will be encouraged to evaluate and improve your own performance, as you would in the workplace.

For each unit you complete you will be awarded a pass (P), merit (M), or distinction (D) grade. You will also be awarded an overall grade, such as M, PP, MMP or DDD.

Each overall grade is equivalent to A levels:

- Certificate – one AS level
- Subsidiary Diploma – one A level
- Diploma – two A levels
- Extended Diploma – three A levels.

And each carries points on the UCAS tariff (see later in this chapter).

BTEC Nationals can lead to:

- employment
- an Advanced Apprenticeship
- higher education – normally in a closely related subject area.

Edexcel is the awarding body. Their website www.edexcel.com gives more information.

Sample programme

(Please note, however, that under the Qualifications and Credit Framework (QCF) being developed in 2010, the structure and content of courses may be changing.)

Edexcel level 3 BTEC National Diploma in construction and the built environment

Mandatory units (ten credits each):

- health, safety and welfare in construction and the built environment
- sustainable construction
- mathematics in construction and the built environment
- science and materials in construction and the built environment
- construction technology and design in construction and civil engineering
- building technology in construction.

Optional units A (ten credits each):

- project management in construction and the built environment
- graphical detailing in construction and the built environment
- measuring, estimating and tendering processes in construction and the built environment
- surveying in construction and civil engineering
- setting out processes in construction and civil engineering
- the underpinning science for the provision of human comfort in buildings
- building surveying in construction
- mechanical and electrical services in construction
- building regulations and control in construction
- computer-aided drafting and design for construction
- further mathematics in construction and the built environment
- property valuation in construction
- project in construction and the built environment
- design procedures in construction
- planning procedures in construction
- property law in construction
- geographical information systems in construction
- surveying technology in construction and civil engineering
- topographic surveying in construction and civil engineering
- employment framework in the built environment
- personal and professional development in the built environment
- information and communication technology in construction and the built environment.

Optional units B (ten credits each):

- conversion and adaptation of buildings

- principles and applications of management techniques in the construction industry

- tendering and estimating in construction

- measurement techniques in construction

- structural behaviour and detailing for construction

- construction design technology

- civil engineering construction.

Units may be studied in any combination, but no more than 30 credits (3 units) may be from optional units B.

Ben chose a BTEC National Diploma in performing arts

He loves the theatre, but is less interested in acting than in stage management or directing.

'I didn't want to do A level drama because I thought that it would be too theoretical and all the study of set texts wouldn't interest me very much. This course is very time consuming because there is a lot of practical work and we are always rehearsing something. I have directed two college plays now – which will look very good on my CV. An option that I didn't expect to get is the module in writing. I'm working hard to improve in this area because scriptwriting is now another area that interests me.'

Muna chose a BTEC National Diploma in public service

'I'm pretty sure that I want to join the police force as soon as I can. But I am too young at the moment and this course is a very good way of filling the time until I can apply. Even when I reach the minimum age I might not get in straightaway because my local force likes you to be a bit older and to have some relevant experience. I might get a job at the end of this course and apply to work as a special constable, or I could also think about applying to be a community support officer with the police.

One of the advantages of the course, though, is that I haven't closed off many options. My personal adviser told me that I will be able to use the qualification to do a higher level course in a related area in higher education. My family would prefer that – so by doing this programme I am keeping everyone happy for the moment! I could perhaps choose one of the Armed Forces – which we also study, but I really don't think that is what I want. Something that has begun to interest me is the work of a paramedic. I am taking options in 'Dealing with accidents' and 'Major incidents' so that I can find out more. I am doing a major project on the police and I want to do a work experience placement there, but I am going to ask whether it is possible to do a placement with paramedics too.'

Yasmin chose an Extended Diploma in media studies

'This is such a wide area that I wanted to start to study it in depth. It ranges over so many things – from broadcast media to the written word and various aspects of art and design. I could have done A levels in communication, English or media studies – but I didn't want a broad-based course. I'm quite focused and I thought that if I didn't start to narrow down my options now I never would!

As far as careers go I keep switching from hoping to get into television to concentrating on print journalism. I'm not interested in news so being a newspaper reporter doesn't attract me. But I am interested in magazine work and I have taken all the options I can in things like print genres, print production, layout and journalistic writing techniques. We also study photography – but I am slowly becoming convinced that what I want is fashion journalism. I know that there are some degree courses in this and I am going to look into them.'

Alex is doing a level 3 Diploma in sport plus an A level in biology

'Everybody knows that I am sports mad. I spend all my spare time in sport-related activities. I am in college football and tennis teams, which play other colleges on Wednesday afternoons. You have to take this seriously, and so there is no time to do other sports at team level. I make up for this by playing for a hockey team on Saturdays in winter. Even my part-time job is at a leisure centre. I'm a general assistant and do everything from setting up and clearing away equipment, to working as a lifeguard or helping to run children's parties.

So it's no surprise that I have chosen these subjects. I chose the combination deliberately because I am fairly certain that I want to go on to a Higher Diploma or degree course in leisure or sports centre management. The A level biology is to give me a more in-depth knowledge of science. This should help my applications. It will also be useful if I decide that I want to teach sport. Again it will help my applications – but will also give me a second teaching subject.'

NVQ courses

At some colleges it is possible to do courses leading to NVQ level 3 in areas like administration, beauty therapy, hospitality or care. Although they can lead to higher education, many students prefer the alternative routes of obtaining higher level NVQs in the workplace or through an Advanced Apprenticeship or taking a part-time foundation degree course. It is usual to do these programmes after completing a relevant level 2 course.

N.B. Under the Qualifications and Credit Framework (QCF) being introduced during 2010, NVQs will be changing and differently named. See Chapter four for more about the QCF.

NVQ level 3 programme in beauty therapy (full-time, one-year course)

The course consists of mandatory, optional and additional modules:

- advanced make-up techniques
- advanced nail techniques
- anatomy and physiology
- aromatherapy
- body massage
- electrical face and body treatments
- epilation
- health, safety and security in the salon
- maintaining and improving services to clients
- work experience.

Assessment

Continuous on-course assessment involving:

- practical observations

- externally set written modular tests

- oral questioning

- completion of projects and workbooks

- production of a portfolio of evidence, which will be subject to external verification.

You are required to take part in the college's work experience programme during your course of study. A work placement or part-time employment within the beauty industry would be advantageous.

Diplomas

Although 'Diploma' is a word used for many different qualifications, in this section it refers to the new (2009–10) Diplomas that are available in England for students aged 14 to 19. They have been developed in collaboration with employers and are being introduced in all areas – you may even be involved in one already in year 10 and 11.

There are Diplomas in:

- business, administration and finance

- construction and the built environment

- creative and media

- engineering

- environmental and land-based studies

- hair and beauty studies

- hospitality

- IT

- manufacturing and product design

- public services

- retail business

- society, health and development

- sport and active leisure
- travel and tourism.

They are a mix of classroom work and practical hands-on, work-related learning. Some of the learning is outside the classroom. Diplomas can be based in a school or college and typically one day a week is spent on another site: at a local college, with a training provider or in another school.

Each one is a two-year course, available at three levels.

Level	Equivalent to	NQF* level
Advanced	3.5 A levels	3
Higher	7 GCSEs A*-C	2
Foundation	5 GCSEs grades D-G	1

*National Qualifications Framework – see Chapter four.

There is also a Progression Diploma (equivalent to 2.5 A levels).

Diplomas are a mix of existing qualifications and some new ones.

- Functional skills – the basic English, maths and ICT we all need for everyday life (Chapter two has more about functional skills).

- Principal learning – about your chosen diploma subject.

- Additional and specialist learning – options you can pick. They could be a GCSE or an A level (depending on which level Diploma you are doing).

- Personal, learning and thinking skills – essential skills we all need to get along such as team working, being creative, study skills and organisational skills (more about these in Chapter two).

- Project or Extended Project – on a subject that interests you.

- Work experience – with an employer related to your Diploma subject.

You can find out more about Diplomas at www.direct.gov.uk/diplomas.

Ashleigh and Sean are taking the Advanced Diploma in business, administration and finance in the sixth form

Ashleigh says, 'It's good because there's so much that's practical. I wanted to stay at school but I didn't like the idea of an academic course. For one of our projects we set up a business. Ours is making and selling puddings. Some of the assignments we do on our own – we each had to write a business plan, then we worked together on a marketing plan. We went along to a local business to do a sales pitch. They told us they wouldn't buy our product, but gave us some tips for next time.'

Sean says, 'I like the way we get out of the classroom so much. We've been to companies and universities, usually at least one trip for each assignment. At the moment we are fixing up work placements. I'm going to the local paper for two weeks. One day a week we go to the learning centre at another school. They've got better IT facilities – more resources and the software we need, with a technician to help us.'

Keri and Alix are doing the Higher Diploma in hair and beauty studies at college

Keri says, 'I was going to do the NVQ level 2 in hairdressing but this is better because I'm doing hair and beauty so I can decide which I like best. We do hand treatments and nails too. And this course has more theory – history, science, anatomy and physiology, business and salon systems. And I love my placement each week in the salon. I'm on reception and if there's nothing to do, the manager told me to read fashion and hair magazines so I can learn all the new trends.'

Alix says, 'The additional learning we're doing is great. We've done perming, setting, blow drying and hair up. We have to bring in our own clients. My mum's been in and my nan. I was nervous doing their hair, but I had the tutor there I could ask. The speakers that come in have been good too. We had one from a spa and from a company that sells all organic hair products. I like hearing about the business side.'

Level 3 work-related qualifications and higher education

All the level 3 courses described here carry UCAS tariff points for university entry (see Chapter five for more about this).

However, as explained in Chapter five, universities set their own entrance requirements and some ask for extra qualifications alongside these work-related ones – usually an A level.

It is quite common, therefore, for students aiming for university to study an A level alongside their Diploma or BTEC National. Here are some examples:

- Advanced Diploma in engineering with maths A level for a student aiming for an engineering degree
- Advanced Diploma in business, administration and finance with accountancy A level for students who want to study accountancy
- BTEC National in sport with A level biology to study sports science or physiotherapy.

You can check the requirements of individual universities and colleges of higher education:

- on the UCAS website, www.ucas.ac.uk
- in individual prospectuses
- on universities' and colleges' own websites.

Other options

Maybe you're not ready to study at level 3? Perhaps your GCSE results were disappointing and you got D-Gs rather than A-Cs? Maybe you missed out on some school because you were ill? Perhaps you have special circumstances that got in the way of finishing year 11?

It's a pity if anyone's education is interrupted for whatever reason, but it's never too late!

Even if you're 15/16 and have reached the end of compulsory education without a level 2 qualification (the equivalent of five GCSEs at grades A*-C), you can still continue with your education and progress onward into the career of your choice.

There are plenty of level 2 qualifications you can take, including a whole range of vocational (work-related) courses. They are available mainly at further education colleges.

Applied GCSEs

These relate to particular occupational areas and can be mixed and matched with other, academic GCSEs. For example, you may want to do English or maths GCSE. Applied GCSEs are very practical and you learn by doing, with more coursework than exams.

The subjects available are:

- art and design
- business
- ICT
- science
- engineering
- health and social care
- leisure and tourism
- manufacturing.

Each one is a double award, equivalent to two GCSEs. Grades are the same as academic GCSEs – A*A* to GG.

OCR and Edexcel BTEC level 2 qualifications

There are OCR and BTEC qualifications at level 2 as well as level 3.

BTEC First Diplomas are similar in structure and content to the National Diplomas. Both these and OCR level 2 Nationals equate to four GCSEs at A*-C, they take one year to complete and are offered in broad work-related areas.

Kate chose the BTEC First in travel and tourism

'My friends think that I am lucky because I have my future all mapped out! My long-term goal is to become an air stewardess, but I am too young at the moment. I also know from my careers adviser that I will need some kind of experience in working with the public before any airlines will consider me. He told me that languages are not as necessary nowadays as they once were, because airlines recruit from all the countries within the European Union – and further afield – and they make sure that they have crews on board who can speak several languages between them. He did say that knowing another

language could still be an advantage when I come to apply, though, so I am going to start Spanish evening classes next year. That's if I get GCSE maths this year. The college is letting me re-sit that because a lot of travel and tourism companies apparently want it in addition to a First Diploma. If I need to take it again I won't have time for Spanish. Fingers crossed!

At the end of this year I have to review my options. I would like to find a job in a travel agency, because I could learn a lot more about the travel business and improve my customer service skills too. The course I'm doing is very good for that. I especially liked some lessons where we had to role-play dealing with difficult customers! My careers adviser has suggested that I might be able to get an Advanced Apprenticeship with a travel agency. My parents, though, want me to stay on. They think I ought to get higher level qualifications. I have promised to apply for a BTEC National course, but I don't really want to have to do it. I haven't rejected it completely though – and my Mum has pointed out that I might not get my dream job, and that it could be wise to have something to fall back on that could help me to do something else in tourism. I think she is a pessimist – but she might be right...'

Stephen is doing an OCR level 2 award in sport

'I had a part-time job at the leisure centre last year – nothing special, mainly moving equipment and directing people to the right courts and so on. While I was there I did some fitness classes and I became really interested in that side of sport and fitness. I asked about getting a full-time job there, but there weren't any coming up. I decided to do this course and continue working at the centre some evenings and weekends so that the manager doesn't forget me.

I thought that I wanted to be a fitness instructor or personal trainer – and I might still find out what specialist qualifications I would need for that. I should have a good start by doing the units I'm taking this year in anatomy, physiology and injury prevention. But I'm also becoming more interested in sports development work since I've done the sports leadership module. I do like football and swimming, and it would be cool to have a job where you got other people interested in what you enjoy. I don't know now whether to *look for a job next year or take another course. I know I shall have to decide soon – but before I did this course I didn't know that there were so many options!'*

Other level 2 courses

There are many other options available at level 2. Some of them are short courses – perhaps 16 or 18 weeks, for two or three days a week. This means you could combine them with other things, maybe other courses or a part-time job. Many colleges and sixth form colleges have a wide range of these types of courses. Here are a couple of examples.

Shanice is taking a level 2 Certificate in administration

'We started this course two weeks ago. I thought I wanted to do hairdressing so I started my level 1 and worked in a salon at weekends. I didn't like it at all, it wasn't what I expected so I changed my mind and did customer service level 1. My tutor has really supported me and helped me settle down. I know what I want to do now – be a hotel receptionist, in the city centre. I don't mind travelling in each day. I want to wear a smart uniform and have my name on a badge. I'd like a job with one of the big international chains. That way, maybe I can go and work abroad.

I've applied for the front office and reception course in September, but this course is a great start. It's only a short course but I've learned so much that will be useful. Last week I did a PowerPoint presentation. I never imagined I'd be able to do that. And I used to pick up the phone and not know what to say. Now I can answer the phone and sound very businesslike. Doing customer service isn't wasted. It got me on this course and I'll need to know how to deal with the customers when I'm working in a hotel.'

Grant is doing a level 2 Certificate in retail and customer service

'I've decided I want to go into retail so this course is a good start on the way. I've worked in a record shop so I've got some practical experience. This qualification will back that up. We do a lot of team work here. I know that's important in a shop. We had to come up

with Christmas card designs together and work on a marketing strategy. We have to do a placement as part of this course. It's like applying for a real job. We have to phone up companies and see if they take students on placements and then go for an interview. I'd like to be a store manager. I'm trying to decide whether it's better to go straight in onto the shop floor or whether I should go into higher education and apply for a management training programme.'

Foundation Learning

Level 1 and entry level courses

Not everyone can manage level 2 courses. If you think that applies to you and that is what your parents or carers and advisers are saying too, then a course at level 1 or entry level might be a good place for you to start. They encourage you to develop your independence and social and work-related skills, so that you can live and work as independently as possible.

The new Qualifications and Credit Framework (QCF), which is being introduced during 2010, allows you to pick units from courses at any level. So you could combine entry level units, level 1 units and even some units from level 2. Chapter four explains more about how the QCF works.

Courses are available in all vocational areas. Some of them are based around specific vocational areas such as food preparation or ICT, others are a more general preparation for working life.

In Foundation Learning you have an individual learning plan to help you get the most out of the course. When designing your learning programme you get lots of help from the people who know what you are capable of – your Connexions personal adviser/careers adviser and your teachers and tutors. They all want to work together with you to help you fulfill your potential.

If you find you are getting on well, then you can continue to take units at different levels and progress to other qualifications – perhaps GCSEs or Diplomas. You may want to aim for an Apprenticeship. (More about work-based learning options in Chapter seven.)

Jamie is on an entry level Vocational Options course

'On this course I'm learning skills that will help me at work. The course is good as it's teaching us so much. First we're in the kitchens learning how to cook – we weigh out the things we need. The tutor says its maths, but it doesn't feel like it! And we're running our own business – we sell cakes and biscuits in the college entrance every week. I think our cupcakes are the best! We take it in turns to serve the customers and one of us does the till. It can be hard to work out which buttons to press but our tutor is there to help. The till tells me how much change to give, but I still have to work out which coins to give the customer. Sometimes I try to work the change out myself to practise my maths.

I used to feel a bit stressed if a customer was waiting but now I just speak politely and they don't usually mind waiting. You have to be nice to the customers even when they are a bit rude.

I feel much more confident now. I know I want to work in media. My tutor is taking me to look at a course in film making, which I want to do when I finish this one.'

Entry to Employment (e2e) and Skill Build (Wales)

These programmes are available if you aren't ready yet for the world of work or an Apprenticeship, or if you don't have the entry qualifications.

From 2010 through to 2013 – at different times in different areas – e2e will become part of Foundation Learning. Your Connexions personal adviser/careers adviser will keep you up to date with what's going on where you live and what your options are. You apply for e2e through your adviser. Before you start, you meet with a member of the e2e programme staff and your adviser to draw up an individual programme designed to meet your needs, to enable you to progress to the work, education or training that you are aiming for. So you need to have a clear goal in mind before you start on e2e. That doesn't mean you need to know exactly what job you want to do. But you need to have an idea which career area you are interested in.

It won't all be classroom based. The programme is likely to include some kind of work-related tasters or placements so you can test out whether your career ideas are really right for you and get some experience in the workplace. You will work towards vocational qualifications at level 1, which will be a real start on the way forward.

Some of the work will be in a group with others on the programme – working on your key skills or learning to work with others. You may go on outdoor activities.

You are expected to attend for 30 hours a week for at least 10 weeks. Different people need different lengths of programme to get where they want to be, so you can stay on e2e as long as you need to – and as long as you are still progressing. You can start on 16 hours a week, but would be expected to build this up to 30 hours.

At the moment (2010), you can apply for Education Maintenance Allowance (EMA) if you are on e2e. This is due to change as Foundation Learning Tier replaces e2e. Again your Connexions personal adviser/careers adviser can keep you up to date.

A typical e2e programme might include:

- a level 1 qualification in a vocational area such as retail, administration, childcare, IT, engineering, horticulture, sport/recreation or catering/hospitality
- work tasters at local employers, which could be for a few days or one day a week over several months
- basic skills or functional skills
- independent living skills including budgeting and cooking
- basic DIY
- parenting skills
- personal and social development
- personal presentation
- equal opportunities
- self-esteem and confidence building
- team work and group skills.

There may be outdoor activities as well:

- outdoor education, including raising confidence and working with others

- sports coaching, with a qualified coach and the opportunity to take coaching qualifications

- a residential, focusing on working with others and including some outdoor activities.

Aimee feels her e2e programme made all the difference

'I was on e2e for six months. I tried the sixth form at school but it wasn't really for me – it's too academic. I'd missed out on going to college so one of my teachers said what about e2e. The best bit was my work placement. Two days a week I was the receptionist at a local training centre. I wasn't just watching someone else do the job, I really was the receptionist. If I hadn't been there, one of the trainers would have had to answer the phone. I could feel my confidence growing over the three months I was there. Now I want to get a job in an office so I'm going to college to get a qualification for that.'

Skill Build in Wales

If you live in Wales and you need work-related training or you are not sure which career direction you want to take, Skill Build can offer work taster placements to help you decide. The programme includes:

- motivational classes

- confidence building

- basic skills

- job-search skills

- work-related learning (which can be at level 1, 2 or 3)

- pre-employment training specific to the career area.

Programmes are individually tailored to meet your needs. There is no time limit – you stay on the programme until you are ready to move on.

You need to apply for Skill Build through your local Careers Wales office. Once you are accepted onto the programme, you can apply for a training allowance of at least £50 a week.

Summary

- There are so many courses, you need to explore your options carefully.

- Work-related learning can start you on your career path.

- Vocational courses are available at all levels.

Chapter seven

Work-based learning?

"Something tells me you're more interested in the first part..."

This chapter looks at the route of training while working, as shown on the chart in Chapter four. The chapter will cover:

- Apprenticeships
- jobs that include training.

There is also Entry to Employment (e2e) in England and Skill Build in Wales, which are work-related learning with work-based elements. They are sometimes described as pre-Apprenticeships as they are designed as a preparation for an Apprenticeship. They are covered in Chapter six.

It should be clear from earlier chapters that training is important for every job you can think of.

Would you know how to:

- cut your best friend's hair...
- sell cameras to enthusiastic amateur photographers...
- extract a tooth...
- write a newspaper article...

... without relevant training? No!

True, but where's the best place to get that training? As we've already seen, you could stay on at school and start to learn work-related skills by doing a Diploma, a BTEC or OCR National or applied A levels, or you could go to college for a vocational course. Another way to get those work-related skills, though, is to WORK!

And, unlike other vocational routes, work-based learning allows you to earn while you learn.

What is work-based learning?

Of course, getting a job is one of the choices you can make at 16+. Chapter four looked at why you might choose this option. Work-based learning is just what is says. You keep on learning but you're working at the same time. You are learning **through** work.

Apprenticeships are the biggest programme of work-based learning. If you take on an Apprenticeship, you will not be alone. Currently (2010), nearly a quarter of a million people are on Apprenticeships.

An Apprenticeship in England, or Foundation Apprenticeship in Wales, is one of the options open to you after Year 11, but 16+ is not the only start point. Apprenticeships are open to people of all ages. It is quite common to do a vocational course at college and then start an Apprenticeship.

Higher Apprenticeships ask for qualifications which you are only likely to get after the age of 16. There is more information about Higher Apprenticeships in later in this chapter.

So the flexibility is there. If you know you want to do an Apprenticeship after year 11, then you can start straightaway but, if you're not sure, you might want to do a vocational course first (see Chapter six). You'll be even more valuable to the Apprenticeship employer with your extra knowledge.

If you are sure, though – you can get started on a career path now, receive good-quality training and be paid too!

Apprenticeships

Apprenticeships are for people who have left full-time education. You work alongside experienced staff and earn a wage. The training takes place:

- on the job – with experienced colleagues
- off the job – in a training centre or college.

Apprenticeships take between one and four years to complete and you will end up with recognised qualifications. The qualifications vary, but all include:

- a work-related qualification such as an NVQ at level 2 or 3 (sometimes both)
- functional skills
- a technical certificate, such as a BTEC or City & Guilds
- a module on employment rights and responsibilities
- other qualifications specified by the particular occupation.

Apprenticeships have been designed by employers to meet the needs of particular job roles and career areas, so each one leads to slightly different qualifications.

What else do I need to know?

You may like to know that all Apprenticeships are real jobs. Like all jobs, you are entitled to certain things from your employer (your rights). During your Apprenticeship you will get:

- free training
- at least 20 days' paid holiday a year
- a wage or salary. Currently (2010) this is at least £95 a week in

England or £50 in Wales, but some employers pay more than this. The average pay is £170 a week. Many employers increase the pay each year. (Pay in the agricultural sector is slightly different and may be lower.) N.B. From October 2010, a national minimum wage of £2.50 per hour is being brought in for apprentices – see under Minimum wage later in this chapter.

This means you may pay tax and National Insurance (as anyone does who works and earns). You might also be given additional help to buy essential textbooks or equipment.

You might also like to know that a 2007 study by the University of Sheffield found that those who have followed a level 3 Apprenticeship earn, on average, £100,000 more throughout their careers than others at level 3.

What is the difference between the NVQ and the technical certificate?

- The NVQ measures what you can do. You learn this on the job and you are assessed in the workplace. It is known as a 'competence-based' qualification.

- The technical certificate assesses your knowledge and understanding of the work. You learn this off the job, in a college or training centre. It may be a qualification that exists already, a BTEC National Award or a City & Guilds Diploma, for example, or it may be a new one that has been developed especially for the industry you are working in. Either way, it is known as a 'knowledge-based' qualification.

(During 2010, as the Qualifications and Credit Framework (QCF) is fully implemented, some NVQs are changing their names. More about the QCF in Chapter four and more about NVQs in Chapter six.)

Off-the-job training

As mentioned above, some of the training is off the job. Some skills are more easily learned away from the place of work. Most jobs involve theoretical knowledge as well as practical abilities. The theory, ideas, discussion and reading will be provided in a separate establishment, but will be related to your practical experience.

Your off-the-job training is likely to be in:

- a further education college, which might be your local college or may be a bit further afield – this will depend on where the course is available and the arrangements made by your employer

- a private learning provider – usually providing specialist courses not found in colleges

- a group training organisation that provides training on behalf of smaller employers where you might train together with other apprentices from other small companies – especially if you are the only apprentice in your organisation

- the employer's training centre – some large employers with big Apprenticeship programmes have their own training centres

- a voluntary organisation that provides training for particular young people – especially those who are disadvantaged or who have special needs.

The training might be:

- day release, one day a week – this might be in term times only if the training is college based or all year round if it's based in a training centre

- block release – periods of a week or several weeks a few times a year.

You might train with apprentices from other organisations (in college or at a learning provider) or with apprentices all from the same organisation as you (in an employer's training centre). This will depend on a lot of factors: the size of the organisation, the number of apprentices, the type of Apprenticeship and the subject of the course, for instance. So it's difficult to say what the arrangements will be for your Apprenticeship. These are things to ask the employer when you are deciding whether or not to take the Apprenticeship.

What can I do an Apprenticeship in?

Nearly anything! If you name a job or career area, chances are there is an Apprenticeship available in it – or in a very closely related area. Currently (2010), there are nearly 200 different types of Apprenticeship available.

A while ago, Apprenticeships were associated with manual trades – motor mechanics, hairdressing, catering, plumbing, farming and so on. There are still Apprenticeships in these job areas, but there are many more in other, less traditional areas now. How about IT, costume design, veterinary nursing and customer service to name a few?

The next few pages give you a flavour of what you could choose from.

But, please REMEMBER that not all Apprenticeships are available in all areas.

There are Apprenticeships across all occupational sectors – probably for every job you can think of, and some you may never have heard of. You are bound to find something that interests you. The main categories are:

- agriculture, horticulture and animal care
- arts, media and publishing
- business, administration and law
- construction, planning and the built environment
- education and training
- engineering and manufacturing technologies
- health, public services and care
- information and communication technology
- leisure, travel and tourism
- retail and commercial enterprise.

There are currently (2010) over 190 Apprenticeships on offer. That's too many to list here and it changes all the time, as new Apprenticeships are created. Here are some examples of what's available in each career area. Each section highlights one or two Apprenticeships to give you an idea of what the options are and what's involved.

N.B. As you read this section, bear in mind that some NVQs may be changing their names during 2010, in line with the new QCF (see Chapter four).

Agriculture, horticulture and animal care

As well as a whole range of jobs in farming, this covers zoos and wildlife parks, environmental conservation and greenkeeping in a golf club or other sports centre. So you could do an Apprenticeship in, for example:

- agriculture
- animal care
- dry stone walling
- environmental conservation
- fencing
- floristry
- trees and timber.

Taking trees and timber as just one example, depending on the employer, you specialise in a particular area:

- forestry – the science of managing trees, forests and woodlands and the production of timber
- timber processing – timber marking, measurement, sawing and transportation of woodland produce
- arboriculture – the planting, care and maintenance of trees and woodlands for the conservation of landscapes.

On a trees and timber Apprenticeship, you take the appropriate NVQ level 2 in forestry, sawmilling or arboriculture. Whichever NVQ you study for you will take certificates of competency in pesticides and the use of chainsaws and other machinery.

An agriculture Apprenticeship could specialise in, for example, general agriculture, vegetable growing, tractor driving, stock, calf rearing, lambing or sheep shearing.

Arts, media and publishing

Arts covers everything from film to fashion and music to museums, as well as the technicians who work behind the scenes, while media covers newspapers, magazines, TV and radio, and the new digital media, too. Apprenticeships in this area fall into two types.

Creative Apprenticeships include:

- community arts
- costume and wardrobe
- cultural and heritage venue operations
- live events and promotion

- music business
- technical theatre (sound, rigging, lighting).

On any of these Apprenticeships you study for a Certificate in creative and cultural practice as well as the relevant NVQ level 2. Community arts, for example, could see you organising and promoting fairs, festivals and fundraisers, using a combination of creative skills and organisational skills. Technical theatre, on the other hand, could involve installing, testing and operating sound, lighting and rigging equipment for performances in theatres and other venues.

Design Apprenticeships include:

- ceramics
- computer games testing
- footwear
- furniture design
- graphics
- interior design
- kitchen or bathroom design
- leather work
- product design.

As a games testing Apprentice, for example, you take an NVQ level 2 in computer games, testing and a BTEC Award in the interactive uses of media.

Business, administration and law

This covers the different jobs needed to keep businesses going including sales, finance and management. Apprenticeships include:

- accounting
- contact centres
- customer service
- marketing and communications
- sales
- telesales.

For example, customer service underpins the whole way in which an organisation deals with its customers. You can do a customer service Apprenticeship across the whole range of business sectors. So you learn about your sector of work as well as gaining a level 2 NVQ in customer service.

Contact centre work is a specialised area of customer service, as businesses provide more and more services by phone. A contact centre apprentice learns how to apply the skills needed to earn the NVQ level 2 in contact centre operations.

Construction, planning and the built environment

This covers the whole range of jobs involved in designing, creating and looking after all types of buildings, from houses to office blocks, and much of the environment that surrounds them, including roads and bridges. Apprenticeships include:

- bricklaying
- carpentry and joinery
- floor covering
- general construction
- heating and ventilation
- plumbing
- refrigeration and air conditioning
- scaffolding.

In a scaffolding Apprenticeship you study for a level 2 technical certificate in access and rigging operations, as well as the NVQ level 2 in access and rigging operations.

In a heating and ventilating Apprenticeship, for example, depending on your employer, there are several areas to specialise in:

- a heating and ventilating fitter installs and repairs industrial, commercial or domestic systems
- welders join pipework in heating and ventilation systems
- ductwork provides air to, or extracts air from, parts of buildings.

You work towards the specific NVQ level 2 in heating and ventilating installation or maintenance for the specialism, as well as the relevant technical certificates, which may be in welding or fitting.

Education and training

There is an Apprenticeship in supporting teaching and learning in schools, to train teaching assistants and cover supervisors. The training leads to a technical certificate in supporting teaching and learning in schools, as well as an NVQ level 2 in supporting teaching and learning in schools.

Engineering and manufacturing technologies

This covers a wide range of industries and occupations including the production of textiles, food, glass, metals, printing and cars as well as making the machinery for manufacture, vehicles for land, sea and air, and power industries. Apprenticeships include:

- aero engine fitter
- avionics fitter
- baker
- boat building
- ceramic decorator
- chocolatier
- coatings
- cycle maintenance technician
- design and draughting technician
- driller
- electricity industry
- highway maintenance
- laboratory technicians
- motor sport technician
- pipefitter
- precast concrete installer
- quality control
- rail transport
- sea fishing
- signmaking

- vehicle body repairs

- watch service technician

- welder/fabricator.

Coatings, for example, involves something you use all the time but probably aren't aware of – the substances that coat the surfaces of computers, walls, clothes and cars, among other things. An Apprenticeship in coatings could lead to an NVQ level 2 in:

- producing surface coatings

- performing manufacturing operations

- laboratory and associated technical activities.

The Apprenticeship would also lead to the relevant technical certificate, depending on the area of work of your employer.

Electricity industry Apprenticeships focus on installation and maintenance of plant, apparatus and equipment, specialising in:

- generation – equipment in power stations

- transmission – working on the National Grid

- distribution – supplying power to homes and businesses.

As an apprentice boat builder, you learn a range of skills including carpentry, electrics, plumbing and welding, as well as maritime skills such as rigging and sailmaking. This leads to an NVQ level 2 in boatbuilding, specialising in maintenance, laminating, marine electrics or marine engineering.

Health, public services and care

This covers a whole range of looking after people's needs – children, the elderly and those with mental heath issues and disabilities – in their own homes, in the community and in facilities such as hospitals.

Some Apprenticeships are very specific, such as:

- children's care, learning and development

- dental nursing

- emergency fire service operations

- installation of security, emergency and alarm systems

- optical

- pharmacy assistant.

Depending on where they work, an optical apprentice, for instance, specialises in either:

- manufacturing – making contact lenses, spectacles or artificial eyes
- retail – working as a dispensing assistant or receptionist in a high street optician.

They take the appropriate NVQ level 2 and relevant technical certificate.

Other Apprenticeships can be applied across the sector for work in different roles with different groups of people, such as:

- advice and guidance
- community development
- health and social care
- housing.

Information and communication technology

This covers the development and use of communications and information technology (IT). You will be only too aware how important computing and IT have become in all aspects of our lives. There are Apprenticeships for:

- IT and telecoms professionals
- IT users.

IT and telecoms professional apprentices specialise in:

- IT – including software installation and technical fault diagnosis
- telecoms – including system security, managing software development and customer care.

Each of these leads to an NVQ level 2 for IT practitioners and a Diploma in professional competence.

The Apprenticeship for IT users trains you in the operation of databases, networks and other applications, leading to an IT user NVQ level 2.

Leisure, travel and tourism

This covers the whole range of activities that contribute to the rest of us enjoying ourselves in travel and sport. Apprenticeships include:

- active leisure
- aviation operations on the ground
- cabin crew
- travel and tourism.

Apprentices in aviation operations on the ground learn the skills needed for baggage handling, ramp-side operations, check-in desks and moving aircraft.

Travel and tourism apprentices learn the skills needed for leisure or business travel, including checking availability, making bookings and processing payments, and can specialise in ticketing, marketing or training. They work towards an NVQ level 2 in travel and tourism services leisure and business, as well as a technical certificate in world travel and tourism destinations.

Retail and commercial enterprise

This covers the selling and distribution of goods and services in shops, spas, warehouses, showrooms, bars, pubs and restaurants. Apprenticeships include:

- barbering
- beauty consultant
- caretaker
- carry and deliver goods
- estate agent
- hairdresser
- mail sorter
- sales assistant
- skin care and make up consultant
- warehouse operative
- window cleaner.

The Apprenticeship in carry and deliver goods covers transport and delivery by motorcycle, van, light goods vehicle or bicycle. You are trained in multi-drop deliveries, customer interaction and, where necessary, in financial transactions for work as a motorcycle or bicycle courier or a driver's mate with an NVQ level 2 in carry and deliver goods.

A hospitality Apprenticeship could lead to an NVQ level 2 in:

- food and drink service – for waiters and barpersons
- food processing and cooking – for large-scale catering in canteens
- front office for hotel receptionists
- hospitality services – for small hotels and hostels
- housekeeping for hotel room services
- professional cookery for chefs in restaurants.

How to get into an Apprenticeship

The National Apprenticeship Service advertises Apprenticeship vacancies in England. The website is www.apprenticeships.org.uk. From the website you can find out about the different types of Apprenticeship and search for Apprenticeship vacancies in your area. Careers Wales operates a vacancy search service for Apprenticeships in Wales.

Then what?

An Apprenticeship is a good start, but it isn't the end of it. As we said in Chapter three, more and more jobs nowadays need skills at a higher level - often level 3, sometimes higher.

Advanced (level 3) Apprenticeships

(Known as Apprenticeships in Wales)

As well as Apprenticeships there are Advanced Apprenticeships, which allow you to develop your skills and work for higher qualifications – usually NVQ level 3. Most of the Apprenticeships we have looked at allow you to go on and study further.

But REMEMBER that this will depend on your employer. Not all will offer Advanced Apprenticeships.

Not every Apprenticeship has an Advanced Apprenticeship to lead on to, so there aren't quite as many as the nearly 200 Apprenticeships we looked at before. There are still too many to list here. To give you a flavour of what's available, here's a selection:

- agriculture
- horse riding instructor

- library assistant
- veterinary nurse
- zoo keeper
- booking agent
- fundraising manager
- logistics manager
- project designer (construction)
- public relations officer
- senior sales adviser
- spa therapist
- stage manager
- team leader.

You can see that some of these jobs have leader, manager or senior in their title. Advanced Apprenticeships give you skills for higher level jobs so they get you going a bit further along that career path.

Again, it doesn't need to end there. Advanced Apprenticeships can lead on to other things if you want them to.

Higher (level 4) Apprenticeships

There are also Higher (level 4) Apprenticeships in some subjects. They lead to a level 4 qualification, which might be an NVQ or sometimes a foundation degree. Here are some examples:

- accounting technician
- aerospace engineering technician
- business analyst
- contact centre team leader
- electrical engineering technician
- IT trainer
- system support engineer
- technical author.

Steve – Apprenticeship in retail

Steve has been working as a stock control general assistant for two years – since he left school at 16. He says that the Apprenticeship will give him a chance to pick up a qualification for the first time, and in something he really enjoys – retail. He has his sights set on a senior management role for the future.

'I get a lot of support from my manager, friends and family, who know how much I enjoy what I do. Although it is still study, it feels like I am building on my real-life experiences too, which is different from school.'

Emma – Apprenticeship in hospitality

Emma works as a trainee chef in a restaurant attached to a garden centre, where she helps to cook the daily menu and is also responsible for hygiene, cleanliness, and health and safety. She likes to get involved with menu planning and enjoys direct contact with customers, some of whom have become friends. Throughout her childhood and teenage years Emma's life has been difficult. She and her brother and sister were taken into local authority care after her mother suffered severe problems.

After finishing school, Emma decided she wanted to be a chef and began working at the restaurant and started her Apprenticeship. Emma knew it would be really hard work as she also had to look after her brother and sister, and make sure that they went to school too. She had no encouragement from her family and was laughed at for trying so hard.

Emma started her Apprenticeship with many personal difficulties but has remained positive, hardworking and determined to succeed. She has now been given her own flat, which means that she has somewhere safe of her own to study and to look after her younger sister. Due to her experience at work, Emma has found that she can help other students at college when they don't understand practical aspects of the course, and she enjoys group work and sharing ideas.

In the future she would like to progress to a larger kitchen where she can learn new skills. She says, 'Eventually I think I would like to be employed in a training role helping others get their qualifications. I would especially like to help people who have been disadvantaged in some way.'

Andrew – Apprenticeship in health and social care

Andrew is training in the care sector with a healthcare company, which employs a number of apprentices working in care homes. Many of Andrew's relatives had worked as care workers, and he knew from an early age that he wanted to follow in their footsteps. But, by law, young people under the age of 18 are not allowed to carry out personal care tasks. This can make it difficult for school leavers aged 16 to 18 to train for work in the care sector unless they decide to go on to college to study for a vocational qualification.

Andrew's careers adviser suggested contacting the company to find out about their Apprenticeship scheme. The programme he is following is organised to allow people to train towards part of a nationally recognised qualification in non-personal care from the age of 16 to 18, and complete the personal care aspect of the Apprenticeship after reaching the legal age required. Andrew works as a general assistant, on the same salary as the other care workers, and during the first two years will cover the technical certificate, key skills and non-personal care aspect of the NVQ. At the age of 18 he will have approximately five personal care NVQ units left to complete. Andrew plans to move on to NVQ level 3 and 4 after completing his Apprenticeship, and eventually become a senior care worker, then a manager.

Thomas – Apprenticeship in transport

Eighteen-year-old Thomas really enjoys his job as an LGV driver, which involves making deliveries across Cumbria and the North of England. At 16 he began an Apprenticeship with a family business of hauliers and livestock carriers. During his Apprenticeship, Thomas qualified as a lift truck driver, gained a car driving licence, and was one of the youngest people in the country to pass the Category C driving qualification for rigid vehicles.

Thomas' training was organised by a local training company. He says, 'At first I was a bit worried about the classroom side. There's a lot to learn about the transport industry, safety and regulations, but the classes are great. We go twice a month and learn from practical materials like tachographs, maps, fuel records and delivery itineraries. Now I've got my portfolio of work, which shows exactly what I can do, and I have just successfully completed the foundation stage of my Apprenticeship.

My mates think it's unreal. I already have my own car and travel around doing a really responsible job. My wages go up as I progress with the company. When I'm fully qualified I will be earning between £20,000 and £24,000 per year – not bad for someone under 20!'

Dale – Apprenticeship in business administration with a district council

Having completed his Apprenticeship, Dale currently works in an administrative role in the Emergency Planning Department of a district council where he supports the emergency team. He also covers the environmental help desk, dealing with issues such as flooding and draining, and deals with enquiries from the general public.

'I had a great sense of satisfaction in completing my Apprenticeship and receiving a qualification. The Apprenticeship has benefited me personally... given me confidence and opened up opportunities that a year ago I would have thought were impossible.' Dale is studying for A levels in psychology and law in his spare time.

Rhys – Foundation Apprenticeship in information technology and electronic services

Rhys left school with (in his own words) 'not very good' exam results, and started his working life with factory jobs that included packing chocolates and laminating, eventually going to work at a textile mill, running textiles machines. Although he enjoyed the work he felt that he wanted to do something more with his life. He started to look seriously at training opportunities and, because he had an interest in computing, began a basic computer course at evening classes. At this time, Rhys' employer offered him a change of job and he began his Foundation Apprenticeship in using information technology.

'I'm getting on really well with the course. My tutor is great and helps me a lot. He comes to see me at work at a time that is convenient, and the work I do on the programme is all work related so I can put it into practice immediately. This is definitely the way forward for me, and I am hoping to go on to an Apprenticeship (leading to level 3 qualifications), which shouldn't be too long now. I am also going to go to night school again in September to start a computer programming course.'

Kris – Advanced Apprenticeship in electrical engineering

'I've nearly finished my second year now. Last year I did NVQ level 2. This year I'm doing the level 3. I'm doing a BTEC National too, at a training centre, every Tuesday. It's a long day, from 9am to 8pm with my journey there and back on top. I like it, though, and the other apprentices come from all over so I get to meet new people.

The practical experience at work really helps with the theory on the course. And there's always someone around to explain anything I don't understand. I think I am working harder than my friends who stayed at school in the sixth form – I have to do my college work on top of working full time. But I know why I'm studying, I've got something to aim for. And I'm earning!

I've been told that they'll be able to offer me a job at the end of the Apprenticeship. I hope so – I want to stay on and get more experience... perhaps even go on some of the overseas projects. Anything can happen over the next few years so I've got a backup plan. I'll go back to college and train to teach sport. Hopefully, I won't need to though!'

For and against Apprenticeships

Like the routes already described in earlier chapters, Apprenticeships are not for everyone. Each route has its advantages and disadvantages.

Some points to consider:

- Apprenticeships are vocational, so before joining a programme you would have to know which job interested you

- you would no longer get the school or college holidays that some of your friends might have.

On the other hand:

- you would be making a start in your chosen career

- you would be earning some money

- you would still have the option of employment or higher education (in your particular field) at the end of the programme.

Programme Led Apprenticeships (PLAs)

You might want to do an Apprenticeship but not be able to find an employer to take you on. A PLA gives you the chance to get some of the qualifications before you start an Apprenticeship with an employer. By starting to gain some of the qualifications, you would be taking the right steps towards your career choice.

PLAs are usually college-based. You would be a student, rather than an employee, but learning things that are covered in Apprenticeships such as a technical certificate or functional skills. PLAs sometimes include time spent in a workplace.

If suitable Apprenticeships become available while you are undertaking a PLA, you can transfer and continue with your qualifications.

There is an important difference between a PLA and an Apprenticeship – on a PLA you are not employed, you are a student. So you don't get the usual apprentice wage. But you can apply for Education Maintenance Allowance (EMA).

(Please note there are plans to end PLAs from 2011.)

Finding work-based learning programmes

There's lots of information available about work-based learning, but how do you find out about opportunities?

Employers want people to take employment or Apprenticeship opportunities so they advertise them. There are lots of places to look:

- Connexions centres/Careers Wales offices
- your local 14–19 prospectus (which will have a different name in each area)
- the National Apprenticeship Service website (in England)
- Connexions Direct – by phone or on the web (contact details in Chapter twelve)
- company websites – if you like the idea of working at a particular company keep an eye on their website, that's where they're most likely to advertise vacancies, or you could ring them
- open days or evenings at colleges and training providers
- local newspapers.

Employers probably won't advertise their vacancies and Apprenticeships in more than one or two of these places, so you may need to keep an eye on all of them from time to time. If this seems like a lot to do, when you're trying to study and doing all those other activities – how about you and your friends dividing them up and each of you looking at one or two places, or taking it in turns week by week?

When you find a job or Apprenticeship you want to apply for, you will probably follow this process.

- Get an application form. This may be from Connexions or Careers Wales or direct from the employer. (Although many are now online.)
- Fill in the forms and return them either to the employer or to your adviser who will send them on. Chapter nine has lots of tips about applications.
- Attend an interview with the employer. You may also have to attend an interview with a training coordinator.
- The employer or training coordinator offers you a place.
- You accept or reject it.
- If you reject it OR you are not made an offer, talk to your personal adviser/careers adviser again.
- When you accept an offer – discuss starting date, time, hours of work, pay, etc.

Starting work as an apprentice or an employee

If you join a large organisation, you'll probably find that on the first day, or even the first few days, you're on an induction programme organised by the human resources department or the training officer. You'll be with all the other new employees – possibly of all ages, not just school or college leavers. The training will include presentations on the organisation and its work, their responsibilities and yours, your rights and benefits, health and safety and possibly a tour of the premises. The training may not take place where you will be working. It will probably be in a training room or training centre, which may even be at a different site from where you will work. It may be a day or two before you see where you are going to work and the people you will work with.

But not everybody works for a large organisation with lots of new people all joining at the same time. You may be starting work at a much smaller place and be the only new employee. You can expect to be introduced to your manager and to a supervisor, or experienced colleague, who will teach you the job and show you what to do. You might have a meeting with whoever is responsible for your training, to discuss college courses or other qualifications that you could take.

Everybody was new once – so if you feel uncertain about what you should be doing, where you should be, where to go for lunch and so on, don't be afraid to ask. People like being asked to help or to give advice.

However high your qualifications when you start work, remember that you are still inexperienced. You are going to be working with colleagues for a long time, and you can help to create a happy atmosphere by remembering that you are the new kid on the block! Don't appear as though you know it all (even if you feel you do) and particularly if you are starting higher up the ladder than people who are older than you are – show respect for their experience. It never hurts to offer to make the tea or coffee either...

Pointers for the first few days

- Try to find out in advance what kind of clothes you can or should wear – the dress code. (You might have been able to work this out when you had your interview.) But if you can't, don't worry. If you get it slightly wrong on the first day, you can wear something different the next day. If you're not certain, it's best to dress up rather than dress down. After all you can take off your jacket or put a tie in your pocket. You'll soon work out what is acceptable. What you don't need to do is spend a lot of money on clothes when you start work. Some smart shirts or tops and dark trousers or a skirt will get you through the first few days.

- Find out how you should address people. First names or title and surname? In most places nowadays, people who work together (colleagues) use first names. But what do you call the boss? Best to ask a colleague, or see what other people do. Be careful though. People who've been there a long time might be on first name terms with senior people, but that doesn't mean that they will want to do this with newcomers. Unless they tell you to use first names, it's better not to do so. They'll soon tell you if that is not what they expect. You can always ask – 'Would you like me to call you Mrs Jones?'

- If you make a mistake (and who doesn't?) admit it, and ask how you can put it right. Don't try to cover up.

- Don't be upset when someone tells you that you have done something wrong. You're at work now not at school, so you're going to be mature and accept (constructive) criticism graciously.

But what if it isn't constructive? Someone is always telling you off – often unfairly? Suppose you have any other problems?

What if:

- nobody seems to be looking after you?

- you don't feel that you are getting the training you were promised?

- you are working longer hours than you expected?

- or you simply don't like the job?

Give it a little while – a few weeks at least. Then, ask advice from a colleague you feel comfortable with or talk to the person who is looking after your induction – your training officer/supervisor/manager. You will probably find them sympathetic and willing to put things right. After all they selected you for the job. They won't want to lose you.

If you are still unhappy, make an appointment for a discussion with your Connexions personal adviser/careers adviser.

Rights at work

There are several laws that protect workers.

The Employment Rights Act covers your contract of employment, period of notice on either side, right to join a union, unfair dismissal, redundancy pay and holidays. (All workers are entitled to four weeks' paid holiday each year, but these 20 days can include bank holidays and periods when the firm is closed – for example between Christmas and New Year.)

The Health and Safety at Work Act helps to keep workers as safe and healthy as possible while they are at work. It requires employers to create a safe working environment, where machinery is guarded, dangerous substances stored safely and protective clothing and equipment, such as hard hats, safety boots and scaffolding are provided. It applies to all workplaces – offices, shops, sports centres, schools. Everyone is entitled to work in a safe environment and be protected from poor lighting, computer-screen glare and so on. There will be accident books in which even minor incidents have to be properly recorded, and details noted of the treatment that was given or steps that were taken. Large organisations often go beyond the requirements of the Act and run positive health sessions where employees can learn about maintaining a healthy lifestyle and minimising stress.

There are laws too under the **Sex Discrimination, Disability Discrimination, Equal Pay** and **Race Relations Acts**, to protect your rights.

The Working Time Regulation means that most employers cannot force you to work for more than 48 hours a week. It also covers rights to rest breaks during the day.

Entitlement to time off for study and training (TfST) applies to you if you are 16 or 17 and have not yet gained level 2 qualifications (five GCSEs at A*-C or equivalent, such as NVQ level 2). You could be eligible for time to be spent on training up to level 2. This could be done in your workplace, part-time at college or through time off to study by distance learning.

The amount of time that you can have off will depend on your circumstances, taking into account the requirements of the course or training as well as your employer's business needs, and you'll be entitled to payment for your time off at the appropriate hourly rate.

But the law is rather vaguely worded. It talks of *reasonable* and *unreasonable*. What exactly do these words mean? It's best to get clarification from a Connexions personal adviser/careers adviser.

Minimum wage

This sets minimum hourly rates of pay for people of different ages:

- £3.64 an hour for workers aged 16 to17
- £4.92 an hour for workers aged 18 to 20
- £5.93 an hour for workers aged 21 and over.

(The rates are revised each year in October. The rates quoted apply from October 2010.)

From October 2010 there is also a minimum wage of £2.50 for apprentices. This applies to:

- apprentices aged 18 and under
- apprentices 19 or over, for the first 12 months of their training.

Good employers abide by all the laws regarding workers' rights. If you need any help because you have a problem with any of them go to see your personal adviser/careers adviser or contact Citizens Advice.

Responsibilities

Yes, with rights come responsibilities. Obviously you must not do anything at work that would endanger other people. You must also take good care of any equipment you use, and do any assignments or other tasks that are required as part of your work or training. And it goes without saying that you must turn up for work punctually – unless you have a good reason (in which case you should do your best to let your manager or supervisor know).

You and money

One of the great things about starting work is having some money (until you see how fast it can disappear, that is!). You may be paid in cash in a wages envelope that shows the gross amount of your pay with deductions taken from it or – as many employers prefer to do today – your salary may be paid directly into your bank account and at the end of each month you will receive a salary notification slip showing how much has been paid in for you – and again what deductions have been made. Deductions? Yes, before you even get your hands on the money the government will have taken its share! You will already have paid income tax and National Insurance contributions. If you start work after leaving higher education you may find that deductions for repayment of a student loan have also been made.

All this means that you might get a bit of a shock at first, and be left with less than you expected to have. On top of that come expenses. You'll probably have fares to pay for and you may have to contribute to household expenses, even if you live at home.

REMEMBER too that if you are paid monthly, you may have to wait to be paid. In most places all employees are paid on the same day each month (often at the end of the month) so how long you have to wait will depend on what date you started.

So, by all means celebrate your first pay packet by treating yourself to some new clothes or a DVD, but it really does pay to work out a budget. This simply means looking at your 'take home' pay – the actual pay you get in your hand, that is – and subtracting from it all the essential things that have to be paid for. These can include clothes for work, bus or train fares and lunches. What's left is yours! But the other part of budgeting involves planning ahead for things you know you'll have to pay for – holidays, presents or a big night out.

After a few months you'll be able to see how the money works out and you may even be able to save long-term – for that car, perhaps.

Summary

- There are Apprenticeships in all career areas.
- Apprenticeships can be at different levels.
- Getting and starting a job or Apprenticeship can be daunting, but people are there to help you through the process.

Some of the case studies for this chapter were provided by the former Learning and Skills Council.

Chapter eight

Where can you study?

"So will you be staying on at school, or ..."

Chapters five and six looked at staying in education – whether academic, work-related or a combination of both. The other part of the decision is where to study.

You may be asking yourself whether you want to:

- stay at school in the sixth form?

- go to a sixth form college?

- go to a further education (FE) college?

But there may be other options too, such as:

- move to another school sixth form?

- stay in your own school sixth form and take some of your courses elsewhere?

What is studying like after the age of 16?

It will be very different because, for the first time, you have control over what you study. Yes, you had some choice of subjects for year 10 and 11, but at 16+ you can chose from a much wider range and, more importantly, it is your choice whether or not you want to study.

Now you have this whole new world in front of you.

- There are many more courses to choose from. There will be lots of courses you have never heard of, as well as some in subjects you have done before.

- You should have a chance to specialise and concentrate in depth on the subjects that mean most to you.

- You will have considerable freedom in the way you work. Your teaching groups are likely to be small and more like discussion groups between you, the other students and the teachers, who may be known as lecturers or tutors. But freedom also means taking responsibility – for planning your work schedule and getting your assignments done.

- You will be beyond the age of compulsory education so the motivation to attend will come from you.

- There are opportunities for leadership and responsibility, which you might not have had before. You might become a prefect in your school sixth form. In a college there will be opportunities to be course rep, be elected to a students' union position or help organise college societies and clubs.

In every decision we make, there are points for and against. Making a decision about your next step is a very personal business.

Further education colleges

Further education (FE) refers to learning beyond the end of compulsory education but not at degree level (which is known as higher education or HE). Most people in FE are aged 16 to 19, but it refers to the level of education, not the age, which is why you may find adults studying in FE colleges (sometimes known as colleges of further education).

Many FE colleges now teach higher education (university level) courses as well.

But you might see some other names. What are they?

- Sixth form colleges – originally for 16- to 19-year-olds, many now offer courses for all ages.

- Tertiary colleges – the word comes from the same place as 'three', referring to the stage of education beyond secondary. Most offer a range of academic and/or work-based courses.

Some are found in particular parts of the country to support local industries.

- Land-based colleges – specialise in courses for those who want to work on the land. In some rural areas they are the only college, so many also offer academic courses.

- Maritime colleges – specialising in courses related to sea-based and offshore work.

Others teach a very specialised range of courses.

- Colleges of technology – with a strong tradition in science, engineering and technology courses – although many now offer a full range of courses.

- Colleges of art – teach mainly art and design.

- Colleges of music, drama or dance – teach courses for talented performers.

And some meet particular needs.

- Specialist colleges – some of them particularly offer courses for people with learning difficulties and/or disabilities.

Some FE colleges have residential facilities – particularly those in rural areas or those that teach courses not available elsewhere.

How are FE courses organised?

College courses are full time or part time. Most courses for 16- to 18-year-olds are described as full time. In practice, it means you will be in college most days but perhaps not every day. It will depend on the course and how the teaching is arranged. Remember, too, that during 2010 all vocational courses are becoming part of the Qualifications and Credit Framework (QCF) and will be based on credits that link to the number of teaching hours. (See chapter four for details of the QCF.)

There are some other patterns of college attendance – usually for people who are in work-based learning (see Chapter seven). They spend most of their time at work, but attend college for some of their qualifications. They might attend college:

- one day a week – usually the same day each week, only in college term times, though. In college holidays, they are at work all week; this is sometime known as day release.

- for a week or more at a time – perhaps several times in a year. Sometimes this is called block release.

For and against

The lists below set out some of the factors FOR and AGAINST each choice of where to study, so you can weigh them up against each other to see which suits you best. Some points will be more important to you than others, though.

You might have considered all the points listed, but some you may not have thought of (and there may be other factors for you). You may want to use these lists as a starting point to draw up your own chart.

Stay at school		Sixth form college		FE college		Different sixth form		Stay at school with courses elsewhere	
+	–	+	–	+	–	+	–	+	–

Consider each one in turn and see which way the scales tip for you.

Staying on at school?

For

- You know the staff and they know you. (Or might this be a minus point?)

- Stay with your friends.

- Continuity of subjects and familiarity of teaching methods.

- Programme of subjects that fits your previous options.

- Everyone has chosen to stay on, so is (or should be) motivated.

- Smaller classes.

- It may be easier to take positions of responsibility in a school where people know you.

- A school can feel like a community where everyone is working together.

- You may be able to continue with sports or other activities you are already involved in.

Against

- The same environment you've been used to for the last few years.

- Maybe the staff know you too well!

- Less chance to make new friends.

- Narrower range of courses than at a college.

- Still not in an adult environment.

- Even if you don't have to wear a uniform there may still be a sixth form dress code.

- You will now be among the eldest students in the school, but there will be a lot of younger people about. You may wish to be free of them.

- You will be expected to take on a position of responsibility and help to set an example to the younger ones.

What about a sixth form college?

For

- Something new.
- Most of the students there will be aged 16 to 19. (Some colleges have adults in some classes.)
- Everyone has chosen to be there.
- More relaxed dress code.
- More freedom than a school sixth form?
- Teaching staff may be on first name terms with students.
- The opportunity to make new friends, from different schools.
- Wider range of courses.
- Possibly better facilities and teaching resources?

Against

- Too big?
- Settling in might take a while.
- Can you tell whether you'll like it after only a visit or two?
- The freer atmosphere might not suit you. What will you do if you're allowed to leave the college at lunchtimes?
- You may have to travel further than you did to school and pay higher fares.

What about an FE college?

For

- Everyone has chosen to be there.
- A wide range of courses.
- More vocational, work-related courses.
- No uniform or a more relaxed dress code.
- A lot of freedom – you don't have to go in some days.
- The timetable may make it easy to fit in a part-time job.

- Teachers will be known as lecturers or tutors and will probably be on first name terms with students.

- Staff often have direct experience of industry and commerce.

- Good equipment and facilities.

- Students of all ages on some courses.

- New friends from different schools.

- Many now offer higher education courses (university level) so you may be able to start a degree at the same college.

Against

- It may be too big.

- You may not want to be with students of all ages. Are you ready to study alongside adults?

- The freer atmosphere requires a lot of self-discipline.

- Can feel less of a community with so many part-time students.

- Students' activities are usually self-started. If there is apathy about, or no-one has time, they don't exist.

- Help will be around, but you might have to ask for it.

- You may have to travel further to college than you did to school and pay higher fares.

What about those other options mentioned earlier:

- moving to another school sixth form?

- staying in your own school sixth form and taking some of your courses elsewhere?

Why might you want to do that? Well, you might want to combine some of the advantages of staying at your school with some of the advantages of moving elsewhere. For example, you want to stay in the sixth form as you've been at your school for five years already, you like the teachers and are looking forward to playing in a school's A team in your best sport, but you want to do a vocational course that your school doesn't offer. You might be able to take one of your courses at a nearby school, especially if the two schools are working in partnership.

If your choice is an Advanced Diploma, then this may be the pattern of your learning anyway.

Or you may know you want to stay on at a school and follow an academic course, but a nearby sixth form has a wider range of subjects, or offers a particular subject you are interested in or even a completely different academic qualification, like the International Baccalaureate (see Chapter five). You may move to another school for years 12 and 13.

So weigh it up to see what's best for you.

Dom decided to stay on at his school's sixth form

'I wanted to go to university so the academic route suited me. School offered the subjects I wanted to do – maths, physics and chemistry. I didn't really want to leave and start somewhere new. I've know the teachers for five years and they know me. I've had to work hard on my maths, but I know the teachers will support me if I need help. Staying here at school means I can be in the teams – football and athletics, mainly. That's a good balance for the hard work! We have to wear a suit in the sixth form. I like that, it feels professional. I'm not sure I'd have stayed at school if we still had to wear uniform. Our sixth form is joint with the girls' school next door. Some of the lessons are here and some are over there. That's good too. I knew a lot of the girls anyway.'

Jon stayed on at his large mixed school where students from other schools join for the sixth form

'I saw sixth form as the reward for my time in the lower school. I couldn't imagine leaving – there would have to be a very good reason. It's not just the courses. I did so much else. I edited the school magazine, took part in Young Enterprise, was joint Head Boy and on the committee for the annual ball. As Head Boy I showed prospective parents around the school, which ate into my study or socialising time. It was a good way to learn how to manage my time. Over the years at school, I'd made some pretty close friends so when a large group of new people joined in the sixth form it shook up some of the friendship groups. I'd joined the school in year 8 myself so I knew what it was like. Some of my closest friends now were new students.'

Ishani moved from her large mixed school to another sixth form at an all girls school

'I looked at a few sixth forms. I moved here because of the smaller class sizes. The first day was hard. I was quite apprehensive, but I knew I had to mix in and settle down. Everyone was friendly and each new girl was assigned a buddy. I wasn't the only new girl, but it seemed as though everyone else knew where to go. My old school was larger, so that made it easier here. It was strange leaving a mixed school. I preferred that, but I've no regrets about moving. I've still got my old friends at home – and new ones here!'

Jenna changed schools for the sport facilities and courses

'It was a big decision. I have to get two buses now, so it's an early start. But it's worth it. This school has a sports centre attached to it and I can do the BTEC National in PE. I've changed schools twice before so I know I can do it, but it's hard coming into a school. Although I wasn't the only new student, there weren't many of us. Because I'm from another area, I didn't know anyone here already. We had two days of team building and group exercises off site. That helped a lot. It's been worth it, though. I'm getting better grades here and the BTEC is helping me with what I want to do – be a PE teacher.'

Money

Which brings us on to the subject of money. As we saw in Chapter four, you won't have to pay fees for the next stage of your education, at school, sixth form college or FE college.

Depending on your household income, you can also apply for Education Maintenance Allowance (EMA), wherever you study after 16. (More on EMA in Chapter four.)

Books and equipment

Depending on the type of course you take you might need to buy some books and equipment. You will be used to paying for some of the materials at school – perhaps for design and technology.

- Schools usually provide most textbooks, but you may have to pay for some.

- Colleges provide course materials, but you may have to buy a textbook.

- On a work-related course, you are likely to need some specialist clothing – salon wear, overalls, or steel toecap boots, for example.

- You may also need some equipment or tools – a set of knives, or scissors, perhaps.

- Day trips and residentials usually have to be paid for – though some courses have fundraising events for this.

Colleges usually make it clear before you start the course what they expect you to provide. You probably won't need to get anything before the course starts. In fact it may be better to wait. You teacher or tutor can tell you exactly what you need – there may be a particular brand they think is best – and they may be able to get discounts with suppliers.

Your circumstances may mean that you will find it difficult to pay for something you need for your course. Every college has a fund they can use to help students. Your college will have a Student Advice or Student Services department who can point you in the right direction – or have a word with the course tutor. They're there to help.

Summary

- Study after 16 is different – you don't have to be there!

- You may have a choice about where to take a particular course.

- Are you ready to leave school or would you be better staying with what you know?

Chapter nine

Making applications

"Your sporting achievements are impressive, but there's no need for a lap of honour..."

Getting started

When you apply for a job, an Apprenticeship or a college place you will nearly always have to make some kind of application. It could be:

- in an application letter
- in a short letter with a CV attached
- on an application form
- online.

In all of these you will need to put some information about yourself. It is a good idea to look for, and put together now, any evidence of skills and achievements that you can think of to help you do this when the time comes. You may have started doing this already if your school uses a Progress File. This probably has some or all of these in it:

- personal details
- school achievements
- qualifications and credits
- record of key skills/functional skills
- social/sports achievements
- Young Enterprise certificate
- employment history
- personal statements.

But you might have other certificates or documents that can also be useful when making applications. They may be from other activities you do outside school.

Have you got any of these?

- ASDAN or Duke of Edinburgh's (DofE) awards
- first aid qualifications
- food safety awards
- music exams
- sports awards, Community Sports Leadership, life saving
- certificates for any voluntary work you do
- letters of praise or congratulation from events or activities
- reference letters from your employer.

It's a good idea to keep them altogether in one place in your Progress File or a folder.

How do you find out where the opportunities are?

Throughout years 10 and 11, your school will arrange for you to attend events to find out about the choices you can make and the opportunities in your area. These will be in school and elsewhere, such as:

- open days at colleges and other providers
- school assemblies
- options evenings
- parents evenings.

You can also do some finding out yourself. Here are some places you can look:

- the internet
- school careers library and notice boards
- Connexions or careers centre
- local and national newspapers
- Jobcentre Plus
- employment agencies.

You may also get suggestions from people you know, or hear about opportunities from TV and radio. Your personal adviser/careers adviser or your school careers coordinator will help too.

As with everything else these days, the internet can be a good source of information about opportunities. There are some websites specifically designed to help you with this. Each area has an online '14–19 prospectus' giving up-to-date details about your choices at 16+. Most also link to online applications, in some cases you can use the same form to apply to different places in your area.

The 14–19 prospectus has different names in different areas, but you will be able to find out about it from your Connexions personal adviser/ careers adviser.

Connexions Direct www.connexions-direct.com has a local services finder, which will give the website of your local 14–19 prospectus if you live in England.

Careers Wales www.careerswales.com will do the same if you live in Wales.

There is more about sources of information in Chapter twelve.

Keeping track

Finding a job or Apprenticeship, or getting a place on a course takes time. You may have to wait to hear from employers, colleges, etc. In order to keep your options open, you will probably be applying for several choices at the same time so you may be waiting to hear back from more than one.

It pays to be organised so you know who you have applied to and where you sent which application. It's a good idea to keep a record of any applications you make, especially if you are applying to several places at the same time. You don't want to forget who you sent which letter to!

As well as keeping copies of forms and letters you send off, why not keep a chart showing how your applications go.

Job/ course	Source	Date of application	Date of reply	Date of interview	Notes
1					
2					
3					

Applying by letter

Your letter of application is your ambassador. It goes before you, and one look at it will tell the reader a great deal about you. It's like putting yourself in an envelope and sending yourself for selection. So it's worth getting it right.

You want to be considered for a job. This is the art of getting noticed. But you want to be noticed for the right reasons – because your letter is neat, well written and full of the right information. Many people will be ignored because they didn't take enough care with their letter of application. Don't let this happen to you. Here are a few tips.

- If you can, write your letter on the computer. Most letters nowadays are written this way.

- Use only plain white paper.

- Plan your layout. As you probably already know, there are standard layouts for business letters – more about this below.

- Think about what you want to say. Use the word processor to add and delete text until you are happy with your letter.

- Put in all the information you need to.

- But don't make the letter too long. Employers get bored with reading too much.

- Keep it simple. You don't need to use complicated language or long words just because you're writing a letter. Have a look at the example below to see how easy it is to say what you mean in a straightforward way.

- Use the spell check. Make sure your computer uses the English (rather than US) dictionary. Employers may not be impressed if you use 'organize' and 'center'.

- Be particularly careful to check that you have included everything that the employer has asked for.

- Remember to sign your letter!

HOWEVER, some employers ask for a handwritten letter. You need to look carefully for specific requests like this. If you don't follow them, an employer probably won't even consider your application. (If you can't follow a simple instruction in applying for a job, how will you be able to do the job? the employer will think.)

Maybe you're not used to writing business letters by hand. Most of the points about wordprocessed letters also apply, but there are some extra points to bear in mind.

- Plain white paper only – no colours, lines, scent or odd shapes. A4 paper is the best size. (Printer paper is fine.)

- Use a line guide if you need to.

- Only use black or blue ink – no bright colours, fluorescents or scented pens.

- It's even more important to plan your layout and what to say, as mistakes will mean starting again.

- Yes, any mistakes **will** mean starting again, unfortunately. You cannot leave mistakes or crossings out in a letter to an employer.

Just think how it will look if you are writing about your attention to detail and there's a mistake in your letter.

- Doing a rough copy first is a good idea – and you'll have a copy to keep when you send off the neat version.

- Even if your handwriting is not much good, you must write the letter yourself (so no getting your friend to write it for you!).

With any letter, hand written or wordprocessed, you may like to show it to someone else before you send it, just to check that you haven't made any obvious mistakes or left anything out.

Any business letter is set out in a similar way, whether by hand or on a computer.

This is the pattern your letter could take.

	Your address and your telephone number (including area code)
Position and address of the person you are writing to	Date in full
Dear	
Subject of letter	
Contents	
Yours faithfully/sincerely	
Signature	
Name written out neatly	

Yours sincerely/Yours faithfully

Are you sure which one to use? The golden rule is:

- when you start with a name you end your letter *Yours sincerely*.

- if you need to start with Dear Sir or Madam, you end with *Yours faithfully*.

It is always better to write to a named person. If an advertisement does not give a name you can phone the company to ask for the name of the manager. If you really can't find out then it will have to be Dear Sir or Madam.

---

74 Dingley Dell
St Peter's Cross
Anytown
TH9 5BZ
01321 447026

18 June 2010

Mrs J. Thompson
Manager
Rip Van Winkle Ltd
76 High Street
Anytown
TH4 3XQ

Dear Mrs Thompson

Vacancy for a sales assistant

I would like to apply for the post of sales assistant with Rip Van Winkle Ltd, as advertised in today's edition of the 'Daily Noise'.

I have recently left St Peter's School, Anytown where I took six GCSEs, including English and maths.

Last year I spent two weeks' work experience in a department store, which I found very interesting and enjoyable. I spent time in different departments including furniture and linens and with stock control and accounts. I have certificates in ECDL and first aid.

My headteacher is willing to provide me with a reference. His details are: Mr P. Wigg, St Peter's School, Ox Lane, Anytown TH2 4BS. Mr J. Bush, Sun Stores, High Street, Anytown TH1 2ET is also willing to be a referee.

I would be happy to attend an interview at any time.

Yours sincerely

Jemima Pondweed

J. PONDWEED

There are several points to stress here.

- Make sure your address is written in full and that it includes the correct postcode. Guessing it won't do. An inaccurate address could cause a delay at the post office and you might receive a request to attend an interview too late. It has happened!

- The title or subject of the letter makes it obvious straightaway what you are writing about. Busy organisations receive lots of letters. You don't want yours to go to the wrong person or department.

- Be clear and positive.

- Try to work out what the employer is looking for. They may make it easy for you by saying in the advertisement something like 'must be willing to learn' or 'someone with experience of children preferred'.

- If you can say something new, it is worth it. You want your letter to stand out in comparison with others, so look at what you are offering to see if there is something distinctive.

- Always ask your referees' permission before giving their names.

- Sign your name clearly. Don't use a flashy signature. Add your full name underneath in upper case.

- Don't forget to get someone else to have a look at your letter.

It is worth making several attempts to get it right, or else it will probably end up filed under B for bin!

So, what is a CV?

CV stands for curriculum vitae – or story of your life, from the Latin for 'how your life has run'. Most people already at work have produced one in the past. Many of them keep theirs up to date, ready to send to a prospective employer at any time. It is one of the ways to apply for a job so you may be asked for one.

It is important that you wordprocess it. Apart from looking neat and being readable, this means you can print copies when you need them, email it to employers if that is what they ask for and make changes to it when you need to.

Here are some simple rules.

A CV should include:

- name, address and telephone number (and email address if you have it)
- date of birth
- name of secondary schools attended, with dates, exams taken (and grades if known)
- positions of responsibility held – in school and outside
- out-of-school interests
- work experience, part-time jobs, voluntary work.

Tips

- Get the dates right.
- Set out your qualifications in full.
- Get your references arranged by asking at least two people if they would be prepared to answer questions about you from interested employers.
- Keep it to one side of A4.
- Write it differently for each job you apply for. This is easily done on a computer.

There are lots of ways of setting out a CV – using different headings and with the information arranged slightly differently. When you first do your CV, as long as the information is clear and complete it doesn't matter which layout you use. Your school or Connexions/careers centre may have a template you can use with the headings already set out.

This is a suggested layout.

Jemima Pondweed		*your name and address in full*
74 Dingley Dell		
St Peter's Cross		
Anytown		
TH9 5BZ		*don't forget your postcode and area code*
01321 447026		
email: jpondweed@mymail.com		

Date of birth | 10th January 1994

School attended | St Peter's School, Anytown 2005–2010

GCSEs recently taken | English   Double science
Maths   Design and technology
Spanish   ICT

add your grades if you've had your results

Other certificates | ECDL
First aid (Red Cross)
DofE bronze

Experience | Two weeks' work experience at Sun Stores –
I spent time in different departments
including furniture, linens, stock control and
accounts

Weekend paper round – I have had this round
for two years

Interests | Youth centre – member of Young People's Voice
School cross country team
Films, reading

Personal statement | I am happy to take responsibility
I like learning new things
I can communicate well with people of all ages

ask permission before you use your referees

References available on request

Covering letter

Would you send a CV on its own? You could do, but the employer may not know which job you are applying for. So it's good idea to use a covering letter with your CV.

This is shorter than the application letter because you are giving relevant information elsewhere. It does not repeat information given in the CV, but it is a good way to draw attention to particular parts of it.

74 Dingley Dell
St Peter's Cross
Anytown
TH9 5BZ
01321 447026

18 June 2010

Mrs J. Thompson
Manager
Rip Van Winkle Ltd
76 High Street
Anytown
TH4 3XQ

Dear Mrs Thompson

Vacancy for a sales assistant

I would like to apply for the post of sales assistant with Rip Van Winkle Ltd, as advertised in today's edition of the 'Daily Noise'. I enclose my CV as requested.

I have recently finished my GCSEs, including English and maths. As you can see from my CV, I did my work experience in retail and I have a weekend paper round.

I am available for interview at any time except the second week in July, when I shall be on a family holiday.

Yours sincerely

Jemima Pondweed

J. PONDWEED

Application forms

This is a very common way to apply for jobs and for some of the other 16+ choices – college, sixth form college and Apprenticeships. Until recently, application forms were always on paper. Nowadays, though, many places use online forms.

Here are some points to note, to help you get it right. Some are relevant for all application forms, paper or online.

- Don't panic! Take your time. You don't have to fill the whole form in at once. You might want to start with the more straightforward sections first – name address, school, etc.

- Make sure you check when the closing date is.

- Read the form carefully making sure you understand all that is being asked.

- Discuss the form fully with someone else.

- Always obey instructions! If it says **IN CAPITALS**, capitals it must be.

- Some questions may look difficult at first – the ones asking you to describe some of your skills or qualities, such as initiative or leadership. They take a bit more thinking about. You may need to practise these sorts of answers. There is more about these questions below.

- Don't leave blanks.

- When the form is finished, get someone to check it over.

- Keep a copy of the finished form.

- DON'T give false information – it will catch you out sooner or later.

For paper forms.

- Make a rough copy before you fill in the final version. Either photocopy the blank form or write your answers out on rough paper first.

- Don't make alterations or cross things out.

- The form may have to be photocopied when it arrives because it is going to be read and considered by a number of people. So make sure your entries are clear, **bold** and in **black.**

- Don't run out of space – this is a good reason for practising on an exact copy first.

- Keep a photocopy, if you can. If not, at least keep your rough notes so you know what you've written.

For online forms.

- Make sure you have all the information to hand before you log on to the application form.

- Remember to save regularly so you don't lose all you've typed in.

- Save a copy at the end. Then you can print it out later (to read before an interview, for example).

Many forms now ask questions that require full answers in reply, such as:

- this job requires qualities of initiative and leadership, please use the space below to describe a situation in which you have demonstrated these skills

- give details of your main out-of-school interests, what have you contributed and what have you got out of them?
- what difficulties or problems have you had to overcome, and how did you do so?

OK, these questions look hard to answer. But they are not so bad really. Not if you go to the personal statement section of your Progress File and look for points there to help you to answer them.

Have you, for instance:

- had a part-time job? In it have you ever dealt with difficult customers? (tact and customer care)
- been in any sports teams? Do you play in a band? (teamwork)
- organised any activities? (initiative, leadership)
- helped at any activities like children's sports? (communication, motivation and teaching skills)
- found one subject really difficult but stuck at it/asked for extra help? OR ever had to retake an exam or test (perseverance and determination – you don't give up easily).

National Apprenticeship Service (NAS)

Searching and applying for an Apprenticeship is easy. The NAS website www.apprenticeships.org.uk lets you:

- find out about Apprenticeships
- search for vacancies, by area, job role, keyword, learning provider or employer
- save your search results
- apply online
- manage your applications by registering and creating your own 'My Home' page.

Applying by telephone

There are some advertised opportunities that ask you to reply by telephone. If an advertisement only gives a phone number, you need to be prepared for an interview over the phone. It may not be straightaway

– the person who answers the phone may put you through to someone else or they may arrange to interview you by phone at a later date.

Think about it. If the job involves using the phone a lot – receptionist or customer care, perhaps – the employer will want to know how well you can work on the phone.

So it's worth being ready.

Be prepared

- Have the advertisement and your CV in front of you so that all the relevant information is nearby. Whatever questions you are asked, you will have the answers ready.

Consider the practicalities

- Try to use a landline, if you can.

- If you are using your mobile phone, make sure that the battery is charged. You do not want it to run out on you mid conversation. If it's a 'Pay as you go', make sure it is topped up. The person you have to speak to may be busy, so you could have to pay for waiting time.

- Have a pen and paper ready to take down any information they give you.

State your purpose

- Always speak clearly and politely, making clear the purpose of your call. Repeat any follow-up instructions (times, dates of interviews, etc) so that there is no misunderstanding later. Then write them down while you still remember.

Think ahead

Plan what you will do if:

- you get a wrong number

- you are cut off within the internal telephone system

- you are offered an appointment you cannot keep.

Remember that everything you say, and especially the way you say it, will be part of the interview.

The interview – Apprenticeships and jobs

If you get an interview, you have passed the first stage and are well on the way. The task now is to persuade the interviewer that you are just the person the organisation is looking for.

From reading Chapter seven, you will know that Apprenticeships are real jobs. So an interview for an Apprenticeship is just like a job interview and just as important. In some cases, there is more competition for an Apprenticeship than for a job (and there may be tests to take as well). So whatever you are applying for, you need to be prepared so you can do your best.

Once again, there are strategies and it's worth taking time and trouble over getting it right.

Beforehand

- Try to find out as much as you can about the company. Have a look at their website. They may also produce printed brochures or booklets about their recruitment.

- Large organisations may send out information with the application form or with the interview letter. Read it all carefully.

- Talk to people who work there or for a similar company.

- Re-read what you wrote in your application.

- Think of some questions you might be asked and try to work out some answers.

- Think of any questions you would like to ask. Write them down and take the list with you.

- Try to arrange a mock interview at school or practise answering interview questions with someone at home.

- Do a dummy travel run in advance to the place where the interview will be to get the timing right. If it is a big place with several buildings find out how long it would take to get from reception to the block where the interviews are being held.

- Decide what you're going to wear.

On the day

It doesn't matter if you're early, but it's very important not to be late. There is no excuse good enough for being late for an interview. So allow a bit of extra time to get there.

Feeling threatened?

Don't be. No interviewer wants to scare you. They want to find the best person to fit the company's needs, and you will be considering if this organisation is the right place for you. The successful interview is one where there is a good fit on both sides. Be aware, though, that there may be more than one person interviewing you.

Nervous?

It is perfectly natural to be very nervous. Your interviewer was probably nervous at their own interview (and they might even be nervous about conducting interviews). But you need to get on top of your nerves when the interview starts.

What the well-dressed job applicant is wearing

The interviewer will expect you to look clean and tidy, wearing clothes that are appropriate for the interview or for the work you may be doing. Remember, you may be interviewed by someone much older than you. Their idea of style may be different from yours. If you can't decide, then it's best to go for plain smart clothes – trousers or skirt with a shirt or top will be fine. And shoes, not trainers. Best to wear something you can feel comfortable in so you can feel relaxed about your clothes, at least.

Listen and concentrate

Make sure you understand what is being asked. If you don't understand, say so and ask the interviewer to repeat or explain the question. Take your time. No interviewer will mind if you pause briefly to think before you answer.

Answer the questions

Be direct, straightforward and, above all, honest. Don't pretend to have experience you have not got. Always answer the questions clearly and directly. Don't be evasive. The interviewer wants to know a bit about you so you need to give more than one-word answers (see the table below).

Start and finish well

Make a good entrance. Be polite and show confidence. Shake hands if the interviewer offers this. Thank the interviewer at the end, however well or badly you think it has gone.

Some questions to expect

- Why did you apply for this position?
- What do you know about the company?
- What are your strengths/weaknesses?
- Why should we offer you this job?
- What are your ambitions?

How to improve your interview technique. Some examples of answers you could give.

Question	Possible answer: true but you could say more	Possible answer: better because it tells the interviewer a bit more about you
Which school did you attend?	Anytown	St Peter's, Anytown – until part-way through the sixth form.
When did you leave?	December	At Christmas, when I made an important career decision.
What exams have you passed?	GCSEs	English D, maths C, biology D, geography D, art C and music C.
What are your interests?	Cinema	I particularly like Ridley Scott films.
How did your work experience go?	All right	I found one or two customers difficult at first, but after I had been particularly upset by one, the manager told me how I could have handled it better. He told me to call him the next time anyone complained, and listen to what he said. I soon learned to handle complaints better.
Why do you want this job?	I want to work in a shop	I enjoyed my work experience in spite of the problems. I think I might want a career in retail.

Rip Van Winkle Ltd
76 High Street
Anytown
TH4 3XQ

15 July 2010

Ms J. Pondweed
74 Dingley Dell
St Peter's Cross
Anytown
TH9 5BZ

Dear Ms Pondweed,

Thank you for attending our interview last Thursday. I am sorry to have to tell you that we are unable to offer you a post in the company.

Yours sincerely
T. Bunkum
for Manager

That's a 'No' then...

So it did not come off – this time

What now?

Be positive

Get the disappointment into perspective. The response that you get is not necessarily a reflection on you as a person. The fact is that Mr Bunkum may have received applications from 50 people, half of whom could have done the job. And that includes you. So cheer up – it's not you who is wrong for the job. It's only that the competition is very fierce.

Keep trying

Don't give up after one or even many refusals. Try, try and try again. The whole business of seeking jobs and landing one is not subject to any rules. What makes for a rejection in one place and an acceptance in another is a curious, unpredictable chemistry of people and places. Above all, don't try to draw any conclusions like, 'If they won't have me at A, there's no chance at B'. There is no logic about it. Each application is a one-off attempt.

Ask for guidance

Get the most out of your Connexions or careers service. Keep closely in touch with your personal adviser/careers adviser so that you are in contact when a suitable vacancy does come in. Tell the staff in the Connexions/careers centre about your movements (like holidays for example).

Think again

Take the opportunity to have a rethink. Are you aiming too high? Are there areas of the country or different careers where more jobs are available? Are your applications good enough? Get someone to check them out and help you improve them.

Look around

Be prepared to travel further from home. The job you want may be available if you are prepared to do this.

Applying to college or sixth form

If you want to go to

- college

- sixth form college

- or another school's sixth form

you will have to fill in an application form. If you want to stay on at your own school sixth form, you may have to fill in an application form too. This may be a paper form or online (more and more colleges have online applications). So the information earlier in this chapter about application forms applies here too.

College, sixth form or sixth form college interviews

This may be much less formal than one for a job and you needn't dress as smartly. If the interview takes place during the school day you'll probably be in your uniform anyway. The interview will be with a member of staff from the course or department you are applying for. Usually they will be trying to find out a bit about you, and making sure that you know about the course you are applying for and that it is the right one for you. They will discuss this with you and may even suggest a different course. It is also your chance to find out about the course or anything else you want to know about the school or college.

This is not like applying for a job when you are competing with lots of other people for one place. But, if the course is very popular there may be some competition for places. Staff will be able to choose the applicants who appear the most interested and motivated.

So, it pays to prepare for a college or sixth form interview just as carefully as you would if going for a job or an Apprenticeship.

You've probably already had the chance to visit on an open day or open evening. If you are applying to somewhere nearby, you may have friends there who were in the years ahead of you at school. So, you will already know quite a lot about the courses, teaching staff and life there.

You may know about the dress code. There could be one, or you may find that students really are free to wear what they wish. Colleges are more likely to have a relaxed dress code – some allow students to wear more or less what they wish. Some colleges only have rules relating to health and safety, for example, sensible soled shoes in workshops and kitchens, hair tied back or covered when using machinery. School sixth forms often insist on business dress – suits, jackets, ties, etc. Sixth form colleges vary – some expect business dress, others say smart casual, some say no jeans.

The interviewer is going to want to find out more about your reasons for doing the course. You might be asked:

- have you a career in mind?

- if so, have you asked professional advice as to whether this course is the right one to get you there?

- what do you know about the course and subject and what steps have you taken to find out?

If it is a practical course or a job-related one you will probably be asked if you have any relevant experience – hobbies, work experience, Saturday job, voluntary work or sports teams, perhaps. These questions aren't designed to catch you out and it won't go against you if you haven't any previous experience. Courses are for beginners – and you will learn all you need to know while you are doing them. It is just helpful for interviewers to know what points about the course they need to explain in more detail.

You might be asked to take examples of work with you (in art and design) or have an audition (music or drama). If you are going to do a course that includes modern languages expect some questions in the language.

There will be an opportunity for you to find out anything you need to know, so why not make a list of questions?

You might want to ask questions like these.

- How big are the classes?
- How many hours of private study will I be expected to put in each week?
- Is there a set number of hours' homework for each subject?
- How much of the course is practical and how much is theory?
- What are the study facilities like? How much access is there to terminals in the study area?
- What books do I need to buy?
- How much of the assessment will be done through coursework?
- Where am I likely to do my work experience placement?
- Will someone come to visit me while I am doing it?
- How much might I have to spend on equipment?
- Will there be any study visits, field trips or foreign exchanges?
- Where do I spend the time when I am not in a class?
- Will I be in a tutor group with students doing the same subjects? With people from my school?
- Can I leave the premises during the day?
- Am I expected to be there if I have nothing on my timetable for a whole morning?
- (If it's a school sixth form) How many other new students will there be?

Toby applied to do A levels at a tertiary college

'The college is a 20-minute walk from my school and they gave me a time and date that was convenient, but they had said that there would be no problem in changing it if it clashed with tests or anything. As I was going there from school I had to go in uniform, which made my mates who are already there pretend to be superior when I saw them in the refectory. I don't know why. The same thing happened to them last year... You don't wear uniform at this college. Anything goes and most students wear jeans.

Anyway I had an interview with a really helpful lecturer. I had already met him as he gave us a mini tour on the college open day. He teaches history. The policy is that you have an interview with someone who teaches one of the subjects you are applying to do, and they are authorised to offer you a place. It wasn't very formal at all. We sat in a corner of an empty classroom and he told me more about the A level course before he asked me why I wanted to do the subject. I explained what I liked about my GCSE course and he said that was good because the A level course covered a similar period. But he did warn me that the work would become much deeper and that I would have to learn how to do a lot of research. He also said that it would be more academic than GCSE, which contained a lot of 'empathy'. I wasn't sure what he meant at first so I asked him to explain.

He said history would be no problem as long as I got a grade C – although higher would be better, and asked which other subjects I wanted to do. I had a problem here. I had already decided on English, but wasn't sure about the other one. I thought I might like sociology, but I wasn't too sure what was involved. My other possibility was politics, and I did know something about that because two of my friends are doing it (and they have told me how good the lecturer is). He said – no worries – and if I would like to go and get a coffee in the refectory he would see if one of the sociology lecturers was free and come to find me. I went to the refectory and that is where I found the students who had been at my school.

The sociology lecturer came in and took me to another table. She asked me what I knew about sociology already, then told me a bit more about it. She was very fair and didn't try to push me into doing her subject. She then said that I had a place, no worries, as long as I got a minimum of four grade Cs and said all I had to do was send a letter saying which subjects I had decided on.

It was a stress-free experience and not really like an interview. The point was that as long as I met the minimum entry requirements I could have a place, and they just wanted to help me to choose the subjects I would do best at.'

Kelly applied to do an OCR level 2 course in travel and tourism

'I was asked if I knew anything about the tourism industry. I did know quite a bit because I have looked up a lot on the internet. The interviewer seemed very pleased and said that not many people appreciated, as I did, that it means working in this country and earning money for the UK, as well as working overseas. He said that some people come along wanting to be travel reps and the course isn't a training for that – although some past students are now doing that job.

He said it was more like a business studies course, but in a particular area. I then said I was rather worried that I wouldn't get a good grade in maths this year, and asked whether I could still have a place if I didn't. I was told that it would not be a problem – but that it would be a good idea to take it again since some employers ask for it. He said there would almost certainly be other students who would want to repeat either maths or English, and the timetable was arranged so that this could be done.'

Martin wasn't sure which course to apply for

'I was hesitating between different types of level 3 business courses. I explained on my application form that I didn't know whether to choose a double A level in an applied subject, a National Diploma, or whether to do general A levels in things like law and accounts. I want to be able to apply for an accountancy or economics degree, but the problem was that I didn't want to give up geography, which is one of my favourite subjects. I'd also thought of the idea of starting economics as an A level subject.

The teacher who interviewed me said that as he taught on both A level in applied subjects and general A level courses he could tell me the differences, and that I could go away and decide what I wanted to do and let him know later. He then said that I didn't even need to do a business subject at all – which surprised me very much coming from him. He said that both the subjects I was talking about doing later could be started at university level, and that I might prefer to keep a wide range of subjects going.

We talked a lot, and in the end I decided that I did want to do one subject at least that would be related to business. We finally agreed a package – an AS in applied business, AS in French (which I hadn't realised I would be able to fit in) and full A levels in economics and geography. That was for the moment anyway. I'll be doing four AS subjects in the first year of my course, and I will be able to decide then which ones I want to take up to A2.

I thought about it for a week, and then phoned to confirm my choice.'

Summary

- Start keeping your certificates in a file or folder.
- Applications can be by letter, form, telephone or online.
- You will probably have to have an interview. It's best to be prepared.

Chapter ten

Career choice

"I can't even decide which careers guide to pick ... "

There are hundreds of careers to choose from and all sorts of reasons for choosing them. Before you can make a choice you need some solid information. One way to do this is to get a good careers directory or look on a careers website (see Chapter twelve). You could then plough through it from beginning to end or flick through it, dipping in and out when something catches your eye.

This might lead you to something you're interested in, but looking through the whole book might take a long time and flicking through might mean you miss something. It might work better to have a starting point.

We can divide jobs into families or groups. We all know what some of our skills and interests are – whether we are very practical, brilliant at science, want to help other people, like to spend most of the day outside and so on. By grouping together jobs that have similar characteristics it's easier to search through just the relevant categories. It's a method of dividing jobs into groups that has stood the test of time. It's still valid, even though the jobs in the categories have changed and developed over the years.

The categories used here are:

1. Administration, business and office work

2. Building and construction

3. Catering and hospitality

4. Computers and IT

5. Design, arts and crafts

6. Education and training

7. Engineering

8. Environment, animals and plants

9. Financial services

10. Healthcare

11. Languages, information and culture

12. Legal and political services

13. Leisure, sport and tourism

14. Manufacturing and production

15. Marketing and advertising

16. Media, print and publishing

17. Performing arts

18. Personal and other services, including hair and beauty

19. Retail and customer services

20. Science, maths and statistics

21. Security and Armed Forces

22. Social work and counselling services

23. Transport and logistics.

You may be familiar with this way of grouping jobs as it is it used in many careers libraries, in schools and colleges, and in Connexions centres. It's also used on the Jobs4u Careers Database, which is part of the Connexions Direct website www.connexions-direct.com. There are other ways to group jobs, but it can help to have the same grouping used in all the places where you might look for careers information.

Jobs don't all pigeonhole quite so neatly. Many jobs have different aspects to them so they could, perhaps, fall into more than one category. Let's take people who write for a living. You might think of the job title 'writer'. That is in the media, print and publishing group. It might seem obvious. But if you look into it a bit deeper, there are different types of writer – people who write in different ways, for different media. There is another job title 'web writer', which has been put into the computers and IT group. And, just for the record, there are also 'technical authors' (who write instructions and technical manuals). Their job appears in the media, print and publishing group, too.

And you might find it hard to decide which jobs are in catering and hospitality and which are in leisure, sport and tourism. 'Holiday centre worker' is in leisure sport and tourism and 'hotel receptionist' is in catering and hospitality. So sometimes, you might need to look in two or more closely related groups to find all the jobs that might interest you. No system of classification is perfect.

What is certain, though, with this classification system no job title appears in more than one group. So if you can't find it, look again!

Within each group is a whole range of jobs. Let's take transport and logistics. Here's a list of jobs in that group:

- air cabin crew
- air traffic controller
- aircraft dispatcher
- airline pilot
- airport baggage handler
- bus/coach driver
- chauffeur
- courier
- distribution manager

- driver's mate
- driving examiner
- driving instructor
- freight forwarder
- helicopter pilot
- importer/exporter
- large goods vehicle driver
- large goods vehicle training instructor
- lift truck operator
- Merchant Navy deck officer
- Merchant Navy engineering officer
- Merchant Navy rating
- motorcycle courier
- passenger carrying vehicle driver trainer
- passenger check-in officer
- passenger services supervisor
- port operative
- postman/woman
- purchasing/procurement manager
- rail track maintenance worker
- railway station assistant
- railway train conductor
- railway train driver
- removals operative
- revenue protection officer
- road transport manager
- route manager
- school road crossing assistant
- signaller

- stock controller/stores assistant
- taxi driver
- tram driver
- transport planner
- transport scheduler
- van driver
- warehouse worker/manager
- waterways operative.

What a variety! One thing they have in common, of course, is that they are all concerned with the transporting of people and goods – on roads, on foot, on sea, on rail and in the air.

Within the group are jobs at different levels, each requiring different levels of skills and qualifications. Some require specific qualifications – helicopter pilot, for example. The law is very clear here. All commercial helicopter pilots must have a licence. To gain the licence they must study a specified number of hours of theory, tested by exams, and have a certain number of flying hours.

Other jobs have age restrictions, particularly in this transport and logistics group. For example:

- you need to be 17 to apply for a helicopter licence
- taxi drivers must be over 21
- a van driver has to be 17 to apply for a driving licence and 18 for larger vehicles
- you need to be over 21 to drive a bus or coach on some routes or to drive a train.

Other jobs in this group have no set entry qualifications:

- airport baggage handler
- driver's mate
- importer/exporter
- port operative
- warehouse worker.

At least in theory, you could enter these jobs with very few, or no, qualifications. But even for these jobs, nowadays many employers prefer applicants with some GCSEs, often maths and English.

Once again, can you see how important qualifications are?

Then you might want to think about the point of entry to a career. There are different levels of responsibility that can be found in most jobs. These can be a starting point when thinking about careers, education, training and qualifications. Which will be your entry level? And, importantly, which level might you reach once you are in the job?

Operative or assistant

People who do more routine tasks in their jobs and whose skill levels vary.

Skilled worker

Skilled people with expertise in a particular aspect of their work but who work under the direction of a team leader or supervisor.

Technologist/technician

Highly skilled, often experienced staff who work with professional and managerial colleagues, interpret their decisions and accept responsibility for certain aspects of work.

Professional/managerial/practitioner

This level contains highly trained people with professional qualifications. They solve problems, lead other people and are often responsible for other people's work.

The levels aren't written in stone. Nowadays, many jobs combine work from different levels, for example a hotel manager may have years of experience and some level 3 and 4 qualifications in hospitality but, in a small hotel, she is likely to take her turn greeting guests and booking them in, which in a large hotel would be the work of a hotel receptionist.

Likewise, a welder is a skilled worker. With some experience he might be a team leader or foreman of a group of other less experienced welders while still doing some fabrication work himself. A workshop manager may even have senior duties such as setting budgets, organising work schedules and taking orders from customers while still doing some of the skilled welding work.

Here are some other examples from different work areas showing typical jobs at each level.

Levels of work	Career areas		
	Business	Construction	Retail
Operative/assistant	post room assistant	construction operative	checkout operator
Skilled	secretary	plasterer	personal shopper
Technician	bilingual PA	architectural technician	antique dealer
Professional/ manager	management consultant	surveyor	retail manager

Some people are self-employed, so they work for themselves, rather than being employed in a company or business. If, as well as working **for** themselves, they also work **by** themselves they can often end up doing everything at all levels! An architect working by herself in her own practice, for example, as well as using her years of professional skill and training to design buildings, may also:

- draw plans using CAD (skilled level)

- prepare planning applications (technician level)

- draft letters to clients and organise her own administrative and filing systems (operative/assistant level).

Where a person's job sits in these levels is likely to depend on:

- how long the person has been in the job (reflected in how much experience they have)

- the qualifications they entered with

- the qualifications they are still working towards.

Not everyone starts at operative or assistant level, though. That's often where your qualifications come in – if you have higher level qualifications you may enter a job at the skilled level, for example, especially if you have gained some work experience through placements on your course or during an Apprenticeship.

For instance, if you do a work-related course in childcare at level 3, perhaps a level 3 Diploma, with some practical placements in a childcare setting, you would not need to start at the operative level. You could apply for a more skilled post, such as classroom assistant in a school or room assistant in a nursery.

With a level 2 work-related qualification in childcare, you are unlikely to be able to apply for a skilled post. You are more likely to start as an assistant – and probably work towards a level 3 qualification in the job. At this point, you would have both the skills and experience to take on the skilled post.

Looking again at the four different levels, we'll take the manager level this time. People become managers in different ways. Some start at one of the other levels, skilled perhaps, and as they gain more experience they are promoted, perhaps to assistant manager then to manager.

It is possible, in some circumstances, to start as a manager or at least a trainee manager. Some large organisations, such as big companies or local authorities, have management training schemes where people are recruited in order to be the managers of the future. They would perhaps spend up to two years studying the work of the business, getting management or leadership qualifications, and working in different departments to get wide experience. Being a manager carries a lot of responsibility for the wellbeing of the business and the people who work there, so companies want to make sure their managers are carefully selected and well trained.

So you can see again that it's all about qualifications.

Here's another example to show how the levels relate to each other, this time from the world of engineering.

Professional engineers develop the concept of a project. They would think through the whole process from idea to reality, manage the project and be responsible for other staff. Job titles might be design engineer, electrical engineer or mechanical engineer. They are likely to have a degree in engineering and several years' experience. They may be Chartered Engineers.

Engineering technicians provide data, information and detailed designs to assist in the realisation of the project. Job titles might be measurement and control technician or mechanical engineering technician. They may have a foundation degree or Higher National Diploma (HND) as well as experience. They may have the professional status of Incorporated Engineer.

Skilled engineering workers use their skills to make and assemble parts. They are responsible for the quality of their work. Job titles might be engineering maintenance fitter or engineering craft/CNC machinist.

Engineering operatives might be involved in some of the more routine processes involved in the manufacture or assembling of parts for the engineering project.

All working together and each playing their part.

Of course, some of the operatives and skilled workers may become the technicians, professionals and managers of the future. This is not just true of engineering, it's also true of other jobs from other groups.

It's quite possible to progress to different job levels. Take the area of financial services, for example.

Let's say you left school after year 11 with some GCSEs. Your grades were OK – you got a couple of Cs and a B, but mainly Ds and an E. You don't really want to stay on at school – you've had enough of that so you apply for a work-related course. You had hoped to do a level 3 course, but the tutor thinks level 2 would be better. You did your work experience in an office and liked that so you apply to college for level 2 in admin.

Your first job is in the admin office of a local company. You're getting on well and after a few months, the manager asks if you'll help out with the invoices – she'll show you how, to get you started. After a few weeks you realise that you are enjoying this more then the rest of the admin. You mention this to the manager who sounds really pleased – someone from accounts is leaving. Would you like to transfer? You decide to give it a go – you can always move back it you really don't like it. But you love it. To help you out the company sends you on a week's course to learn the computer accounts system. The more you do it the more you like it!

You begin to wonder about further qualifications. The website of your local college has all sorts of courses in bookkeeping and accounts. There's a level 3 course in accounting on a Thursday in the early evening. Would they let you leave work early to go on that? You pick the right time to ask the manager about it and she says – yes! They are pleased to have better qualified staff in the company. Some of the course is hard to get to grips with, but you can ask people at work about things you don't understand. The course helps you to see why you have to do some things at work in a particular way. You're pleased when you pass the course. All that hard work to get your coursework done at weekends was worth it!

The manager congratulates you on your hard work and asks if you'd like to become the team leader in the accounts department. You feel as though you're a bit young, some of the staff are much older than you are. The manager tells you she's seen you working and has been impressed by your attention to detail and that your college course has made a real difference to how you work.

One day, a few months later the manager tells you that she stayed on at school and went to university. She studied business and finance. 'I became a junior manager in the company. I felt very inexperienced in my first job. I can see how it's helped you as a team leader to have worked as an accounts clerk. You seem much more confident than I did, even though I had a degree.'

So here you are with your qualification and some experience, in charge of a team of staff running the accounts payable section. Where could you go from here? You'd like to progress further but you found going to college each week after work made it a long day. What about distance learning? You read at college about the Association of Accounting Technicians. A look at their website tells you that you can take qualifications up to level 4. If you become a full member of the Association you could run your own accountancy company!

As well as working in accounts, you're also supervising staff so you start thinking about some training in leadership or management. When you discuss this with the manager, she suggests the NVQ level 3 in management, which you mainly do by being assessed at work. You decide to concentrate on this for now and think about more accounting courses for the future.

So you see how qualifications and experience work together so you can advance in your career.

One final note about qualifications. Some occupations have very clear qualifications that everyone must achieve, usually because the law requires people in that profession to reach certain standards.

Here are some examples:

- doctors

- nurses

- vets

- pilots

- electricians
- teachers
- architects
- solicitors
- barristers.

In many cases there are different ways to reach that qualification level. For example, some teachers go to university to study the subject they are going to teach, and then do a postgraduate teaching qualification; others qualify while working in a school, but all must reach the required level before being registered as having Qualified Teacher Status.

Summary

- There is such a range of careers that you may need to narrow down before you start looking in detail.
- There are different ways to get into most careers and lots of ways to progress.
- Qualifications and experience work together – you need both.

Chapter eleven

Looking ahead – your options at 18+

You won't have finished making decisions at the end of this year! Far from it. If you do a full-time course that leads to A levels, a Diploma, BTEC or OCR National, or gain a level 3 qualification in the workplace, you will have to make decisions about your options going forward – just like you had to this year – all over again.

This time they will be:

- employment with training
- an Advanced or Higher Apprenticeship
- higher education (HE).

In HE you will be able to do a general, academic course or a career-related, vocational course.

Employment

Job prospects definitely improve when you have achieved level 3 qualifications. Even though the entry requirement for an increasing number of careers is now a degree, there are still employers who value the skills you will have, or can develop, and who give credit for advanced study. Chapter four showed some pay figures for people with different levels of qualifications – generally more than average pay for higher qualifications. Some people are much better off with a 'learning while earning' method and prefer this route to full-time HE.

If you choose this route, though, you need to realise that getting a job does not mean saying goodbye to studying and exams. Good jobs usually mean further study, for professional qualifications or a degree and, quite often, you do it at evening classes after a full day's work. You might be lucky enough to find an employer who would give you a day off during the week to attend college – which would be a big help.

What sort of job could you get?

Chapter ten has examples of different jobs and careers, with information about where you might enter and how you might progress. We have already seen how the qualifications you have when you enter a job are likely to affect your level of entry, and that you can study further once in the job.

Nearly every career area has professional qualifications you could study for – and that will help your job prospects and chances of promotion.

Here are a few examples.

Job area	Qualifications
administrative assistant	NVQs in business admin level 1 to 5
animal groomer	Pet Care Trust Certificates and Diploma
contact centre operator	Customer Contact Association Certificate and Diploma NVQs in call handling levels 2 to 4
customer service	Institute of Customer Service Awards NVQs in customer service levels 1 to 4
engineering operative	BTEC Certificate and Diploma in operations and maintenance engineering
foundry moulder/ coremaker	Institute of Cast Metals Engineers courses
hotel receptionist	Institute of Hospitality Certificates level 2 and 3
IT support/helpdesk	Computer Industry Training Association Certificate
leisure centre assistant	Institute of Sport and Recreation Management Certificate Institute for Sports Parks and Leisure Awards and Certificate
pest control technician	National Pest Technicians Association Diploma British Pest Control Association Certificate
travel agent	Guild of Travel Management Companies Certificate NVQs in travel and tourism at level 2 and 3 City & Guilds certificate in air fares and ticketing

Advanced and Higher Apprenticeships

One way you can be sure of good training is to enter the job through the Apprenticeship programmes. All Apprenticeships are open to 16-to19-year-olds and Advanced and Higher Apprenticeships are designed for those with qualifications at level 3 and above – whether those qualifications are from an Apprenticeship or elsewhere.

Chapter seven has information about Advanced and Higher Apprenticeships, and there is more information on the National Apprenticeship Service website www.apprenticeships.org.uk.

That was a very brief summary of opportunities. You can find a lot more detail in two other books. These are:

Decisions at 17/18 +, Lifetime Publishing.

Jobs and Careers after A level and Equivalent Advanced Qualifications, Lifetime Publishing.

Higher education

This is now a major option for people with level 3 or higher qualifications. Over 40% of 18-year-olds now choose it. There are over 50,000 courses to choose from!

What could you do?

- **A general academic degree**, perhaps in the subject you enjoy most or maybe in something new. There are thousands of courses to choose from. They usually take three years of full-time study. Some, for example, modern language courses, take four years and include a year abroad. General academic degrees may not lead directly to a specific job role (unless you want to teach or do further research), but because they are so general it is a way of keeping your options open for longer. A degree like this is a good choice if you enjoy studying for its own sake.

- **A full-time vocational degree.** Examples include architecture, engineering, social work or nursing. They are for students who know which career they wish to follow. Since they include work experience and training they take longer to complete. Medicine takes five years, for example. The degrees do not always qualify you fully. Often, they must be followed by further professional training.

- **A full-time, three-year vocationally related degree**, which doesn't lead directly to a profession like those mentioned above, but is directed to a career area such as management, business studies, marketing or logistics. You may know that you are interested in a broad career area, without knowing where you want to end up.

- **A sandwich degree**. These are in subjects like business studies, engineering, construction and computing. They include up to 12 months' paid industrial experience, so usually last at least four years.

- **A foundation degree**. These are always in vocational subjects and include work experience. They last two years and can be followed by further study to be converted into an honours degree.

- **A Higher National Diploma (HND)**. These are in vocational subjects and include work experience. HNDs take two years' full time, but there are some longer sandwich courses available. They are recognised by employers in their own right, but can also be topped up to a degree. This would take you one year or two, depending on how close the content of the HND course is to the degree course.

- **A part-time course**. Many foundation degrees, HNDs and some degrees can be studied part time (more information below).

Of course, whatever you decide to study it does not mean that you are obliged to follow a particular career path at the end of it. People change their minds all the time, and opportunities arise that you hadn't thought of. And, if you are 16 now, it will be at least five years until you graduate from university. The world is changing rapidly and no-one knows what will happen between now and then.

Higher education is expensive (there is more information on finances below). Most students nowadays take out a loan, which has to be paid back – often this takes many years. So it's a good idea to think carefully about going to university and be sure it is what you want to do and what you need to do for your career and personal ambitions.

If you decide on a non-vocational course, do not worry that this will lead nowhere. Many jobs for graduates (people with degrees) do not specify a degree in a particular subject. What the employers are looking for are the general and personal skills that studying at this level gives you. In Chapter five we looked at the skills you would acquire from a general academic education at 16+. Here's a reminder of what this might help you to be able to do:

- assimilate new information
- bring together information from different sources
- decide which information is relevant
- summarise the arguments
- communicate
- present a reasoned argument
- analyse information critically
- structure an essay or report
- think for yourself
- weigh up evidence and opposing arguments
- reach conclusions and solutions
- manage your own study.

A general degree will increase and develop these skills. Many of these are very valuable to an employer. They will welcome your ability to take in information from different sources and summarise it in a report. In the workplace, the information might come from talking to people or doing surveys rather than from books, but the skills you will use are the same.

And 'managing your own study' translates exactly to managing your own time and setting your own priorities, which are both very valuable work skills.

Types of course
You will be able to choose from:

- single subject, giving you the opportunity to study one subject in depth – sometimes with the requirement to take a subsidiary subject to prevent your study becoming too narrow
- joint subjects – the study of two subjects of equal weight or as a major/minor split

- combined course – with the study of three or more subjects; one pattern, although there are others, is to have a three-subject first year, dropping to two in the second.

There are advantages and disadvantages to each of these, depending on your career ambitions and your personal preference. A joint or combined course might seem like a good idea, but they do not allow you to study each subject in nearly as much depth as a single subject course.

When choosing any course or subject you will want to check with a personal adviser/careers adviser that you are keeping the right options open and not closing any doors too early.

Where will you go?

There are universities and colleges of HE all over the country. When the time comes you'll have your own reasons for choosing. You may want to be in a big city or in a small place, stay close to home or move away. Studying overseas may even be an option. If you're not sure yet about moving away from home, many further education colleges now offer some HE courses, so you may be able to start a degree at your local college – maybe even the one where you are already studying.

Part-time HE

More and more courses are being offered part time. Many students work part time while studying for a full-time degree (see the Money matters section, below). This is the other way round – you may work full time and study part time. The study may be in the evenings or at weekends.

As you may have guessed, it's not easy. But you'd get support from the college or university and you'd be with others, of all ages, studying part time like you. Some employers support this type of study, especially if it's relevant to the work.

One of the great attractions of studying like this is that you are less likely to end up with a student loan to pay back – unlike most people who are in full-time HE. You will also be getting valuable work experience while you study.

Money matters

It always does! Some points to think about.

- Universities UK estimated in 2007 that graduates earn on average 25% more than those who leave school with A levels.

- Graduates can expect to earn at least £100,000, possibly as much as £400,000, more over their working life than those who get a job after A levels.

Going into HE is not free, but there is help available. Some of the help depends on household income and some has to be paid back.

What are the costs at university? Unlike school, you have to pay for your tuition (teaching). For 2010/2011, publicly funded universities and colleges can charge up to £3,290 for tuition. Some performing arts colleges and a small number of other private institutions charge higher fees.

Applications for HE funding are through:

- Student Finance England www.studentfinance.direct.gov.uk
- Student Finance Wales www.studentfinancewales.co.uk

Students from England in full-time HE can apply for:

- a tuition fee loan, to cover tuition fees in full
- a maintenance loan of up to £4,950, which depends on your household income, where you live and where you study
- a maintenance grant or special support grant of up to £2,906
- a bursary from your university or college.

The arrangements are slightly different for students from Wales where, for example, the learning grant is higher (£5,000 from 2010/11). There are full details on the website.

Student Finance England has said that around 40% of students will qualify for the maximum grants in 2010/11, with many more receiving at least a partial grant.

The loan part of student finance has to be paid back, but not immediately. You do not start paying back until you have finished (or left) the course, and only then when you are earning more than £1,250 a month (£15,000 a year). The payments are limited to 9% of your salary, which is usually deducted from your pay (like tax and National Insurance).

The websites have a finance calculator, so you can get an idea of what funding you might get, as well as an online application form and all the information you need.

There are different finance arrangements for some HE courses, such as healthcare, social care and initial teacher training courses. There is extra help if you are disabled or have other special needs, or if you have adults or children who are dependent on you. The Student Finance website has details.

Part-time HE students in England can apply for a fee grant, for tuition, and a course grant, to help with books, materials and travel. The maximum for 2010/11 is £1,495 depending on circumstances. As it's a grant it doesn't have to be paid back.

Other possible sources of funding for HE:

- scholarships from other organisations, such as the Armed Forces, charitable organisations or professional bodies
- sponsorship from companies.

Studies have shown that at least half of all students work part time during term time and even more in the university holidays. Opinions differ on how much work a student can combine with a full-time course. This will depend on the course. Some subjects, like medicine, have more formal teaching hours than others. Research shows that working a high number of hours a week can affect the standard of degree you end up with.

For many students, working is a reality and a necessity. If the work is relevant to the course, it is a bonus. But even if not, you will be learning valuable lessons about the world of work, which will stand you in good stead when it comes to applying for full-time jobs.

Taking a gap year

Some people know they want to go to university, but not straightaway, so they take a gap year.

Gap years can be used in many different ways:

- overseas travel
- voluntary work – overseas or in this country
- to learn a new skill – like a language, by working in another country
- to get some work experience

- to earn money to help finance your HE

or any combination of these.

So widespread has taking a gap year become, that there are now entire books and websites devoted to the subject. You will find a selection in Chapter twelve.

Final word

By now you should have a good idea about what your options are at 16+ and what they might be when you get to 18. There are a lot of opportunities for you to take. Good luck – and choose well!

Summary

- Decisions don't stop at 16. You will need to decide what to do at 18+.
- Some of the choices are the same – employment, education, Apprenticeship.
- Higher education is an option, but think carefully about whether it's right for you.

Chapter twelve

Where can you find out more?

In order to make the right decision, you will need to gather together plenty of information so that you can make a truly informed choice. This chapter contains a list of useful websites, books and events.

You will be able to find the books in your local Connexions/careers centre or in the careers library at school or college.

Careers information

Careers Wales www.careerswales.com

Connexions Direct www.connexions-direct.com
(includes links to the Jobs4u Careers Database and local Connexions services)

Your local Connexions or careers centre website

Sector Skills Councils – access them through www.sscalliance.org

Your school, college or Connexions/careers centre may use

- eCLIPS or KeyCLIPS
- Kudos

Books

A to Z of Careers and Jobs, Kogan Page.

Careers 2010, Trotman Publishing. A directory of general careers information with information on specific jobs, published annually.

Careers Uncovered, Trotman Publishing. A series of books each looking at a particular group of professional careers.

CVs and Applications, Lifetime Publishing.

Excel at Interviews, Lifetime Publishing.

Decisions at 17/18 +, Lifetime Publishing.

Jobfile, VT Lifeskills.

Jobs and Careers after A Levels and Equivalent Advanced Qualifications, Lifetime Publishing.

The Penguin Careers Guide, Penguin.

Real Life Guides, Trotman Publishing. A series looking at what it's really like to work in a career area, including case studies.

Working In series, VT Lifeskills. Each book in the series covers a career area such as finance, work with animals, the emergency services, computing and IT or hospitality and so on – with case studies profiling young people.

Which A Levels? – The guide to choosing A levels, Advanced Diplomas and other post-16 qualifications, Lifetime Publishing.

You Want to Do What?!, Trotman Publishing. Eighty alternative career options.

You should find these publications in your school careers library, at your Connexions/careers centre or at your local public library.

Please be sure to consult the latest and most up-to-date editions of all the above. (Look for the publication date on the cover or front page.)

Apprenticeships

National Apprenticeship Service: www.apprenticeships.org.uk

Finance

http://moneytolearn.direct.gov.uk

Student Finance England: www.studentfinance.direct.gov.uk

Student Finance Wales: www.studentfinancewales.co.uk

Revision

www.s-cool.co.uk

www.revisioncentre.co.uk

www.bbc.co.uk/schools/bitesize

www.projectgcse.co.uk

www.gcse.com

Courses

www.ocrnationals.com

www.edexcel.com

http://yp.direct.gov.uk/diplomas

your local 14–19 online prospectus

Books

British Qualifications, Kogan Page. A guide to educational, technical, professional and academic qualifications in the UK.

Higher education

UCAS (Universities and Colleges Admissions Service) www.ucas.com

Graduate Prospects: www.prospects.ac.uk

Books

Navigate – a guide to options at 18+ with level 3 qualifications, Lifetime Publishing.

Degree Course Descriptions, Cambridge Occupational Analysts Ltd.

Progression Series, UCAS. For information about courses and entry requirements in various subject areas.

Careers with an Arts or Humanities Degree, Lifetime Publishing.

Careers with a Science Degree, Lifetime Publishing.

Events

Careers conventions/careers fairs

Organised by schools, colleges, employers or training providers who set up stands with people to talk to about opportunities for young people and answer questions. There may even be young people for you to talk to – apprentices or students, perhaps.

Higher education fairs

Look out for higher education fairs, where universities and colleges set up stalls and are willing to answer questions about their courses. UCAS staff may also be present to answer any questions on applications to higher education.

Open days/evenings

All sixth form colleges, further education colleges and higher education institutions have open days when you can have a look around, meet the lecturers and check out the facilities. Again, have your questions ready. As mentioned earlier, these are often held in October and November.

Self-employment

Shell LiveWIRE: www.shell-livewire.org

Prince's Trust: www.princes-trust.org.uk

Business Link: www.businesslink.gov.uk

Abbreviations

AEA	Advanced Extension Award
A level	Advanced level
AQA	Assessment and Qualifications Alliance
AS	Advanced Supplementary
BTEC	Business and Technology Education Council, now part of Edexcel
C&G	City & Guilds
CRAC	Careers Research and Advisory Centre
DfE	Department for Education (previously the DCSF - Department for Children, Schools and Families)
ECDL	European Computer Driving Licence
Edexcel	Examining body formed by the merger of BTEC and the University of London Examinations Board
EMA	Education Maintenance Allowance
e2e	Entry to Employment
FE	further education
FL	Foundation Learning
GCE	General Certificate of Education
GCSE	General Certificate of Secondary Education
HE	higher education
HNC	Higher National Certificate
HND	Higher National Diploma
IB	International Baccalaureate
LEA	Local Education Authority
NQF	National Qualifications Framework
NVQ	National Vocational Qualification
OCR	Oxford, Cambridge and RSA Examinations
QCA	Qualifications and Curriculum Authority
QCF	Qualifications and Credit Framework

RSA   Royal Society of Arts

UCAS   Universities and Colleges Admissions Service

WJEC/CBAC   Welsh Joint Education Committee/Cyd-bwyllgor Addysg Cymru

Index

More titles in the Student Helpbook series ...

helping students make the right choices about their careers and education.

Careers with a Science Degree – Over 100 job ideas to inspire you

An excellent read for anyone considering science at degree level.

5th edition, £12.99   ISBN: 978-1904979-39-5

Careers with an Arts or Humanities Degree – Over 100 job ideas to inspire you

An excellent read for anyone considering arts or humanities subjects at degree level.

5th edition £12.99   ISBN: 978-1904979-40-1

Which A levels? – The guide to choosing A levels, Advanced Diplomas and other post-16 qualifications

Features over 50 A level subjects and the range of Advanced Diplomas. Includes career options after A levels/Advanced Diploma and as a graduate.

7th edition £14.99   ISBN: 978-1904979-41-8

Jobs and Careers after A levels and equivalent advanced qualifications

Opportunities for students leaving school or college at 18, including advice on job-hunting, applications and interviews.

9th edition £11.99   ISBN: 978-1904979-21-0

CVs and Applications

For anyone who is applying for a job or college place; includes details of how to use the internet in marketing yourself.

7th edition £12.99   ISBN: 978-1904979-44-9

Excel at Interviews

This highly successful book makes invaluable reading for students and jobhunters.

6th edition £11.99   ISBN: 978-1904979-22-7

Visit us online to view our full range of resources at:
www.lifetime-publishing.co.uk

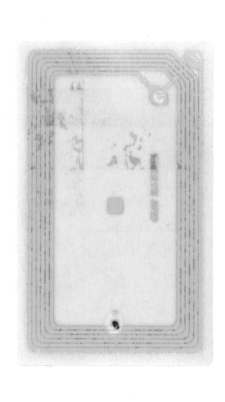